Trees Wear Glasses, Don't They?

A Call to Faith

Debbie Turner

www.xulonpress.com

This book is dedicated to my precious son,
Stephen Ryan Dropps.

When you entered my life,
you filled my heart with everlasting love
and gave new meaning to each day.

When you left me, you introduced me to our Savior,
Who gave purpose to what had gone before
and everything that is yet to come.

I praise God for your life, my child.
I am immeasurably blessed for having known you.

Contents

Prologue

WALK WITH GOD

Written by: Dan Barker, my beloved brother

I walked alone
On a quiet country path,
Cut through a wood
On a cold and bitter winter day.

The sleet stung my cheeks
As into the wind I plodded on,
Through drift and drift
Of fresh fallen snow.

At length I came to rest
Against a tree that provided no shelter
But was something to lean on,
And I was content.

When just as I had stretched
Out my arms,
A most wondrous thing occurred;
A snowflake the size of a silver dollar
Fluttered down from the heavens –

And came to rest
In the palm of my hand.

And here in the wood,
Among millions and millions
Of snowflakes,

I found the One –

I found the One most perfect,
The One most pure –

And I knew it to be a gift from God.

And I drew the snowflake to me
And gazed into it,
And the colors of the rainbow
Danced in the palm of my hand.

And my heart was full and warmed;
I closed my eyes and was filled with peace.
When my eyes were opened,
My joy turned to sorrow
To find but a droplet of water
That remained in the palm of my hand.

And my sorrow bore anger.

And raising my fist to the sky,
I cried to the Lord –

"Thou art a most careless God!
To give a gift most precious,
And allow it to be taken from me
In the blink of an eye!"

And I felt the hand of the Father
On me –

And He spoke to me softly,

"Be still My child,
And hear My word.
Was it the possessing of
The snowflake that first warmed your heart
And not its own rare and natural beauty?

The snowflake knew its purpose
E're I stretched out My hand,
And bid it ride the winds
And seek ye out
To share in its glory.

The love that this snowflake
Has brought to you –

That is My intended gift,
And nothing
Can take that from you.
It is a gift from God.

And I cried to the Lord,
And my tears mingled with the droplet
Of water that remained
In the palm of my hand.

And they in turn
Fell to the earth from whence they came.

And I reached for Him.

And I and the Lord
Walked hand in hand
On a calm country path,
Cut through a wood,

On a warm winter's day.

I waited patiently for the Lord;
he turned to me and heard my cry.
He lifted me out of the slimy pit,
out of the mud and the mire;
he set my feet on a rock
and gave me a firm place to stand.
He put a new song in my mouth,
a hymn of praise to our God.
Many will see and fear
and put their trust in the Lord.
Psalm 40:1-3

Foreword

Do you hunger for perfect faith? Are you longing to possess an unwavering belief in a loving God that remains rock solid despite enormous obstacles and crushing tragedy; a spectacular faith that will send you soaring high above the tallest mountain yet will also carry you to safety, securely wrapped in arms of steel through the darkest valley?

I ask you to take my hand and walk awhile with me. You will witness the birth of precisely that sort of faith. The title of this book, *Trees Wear Glasses, Don't They?*, is symbolic of believing God and trusting Him even when it appears to make no sense to do so. The title stems from an encounter with God that left me convinced that walking with Him in perfect faith is attainable. Bound as we are by human limitations, we may lose our grip on it momentarily. We are weak and falter as our minds struggle vainly to comprehend what is truly incomprehensible – the enormity and awesome power of God. Nevertheless, if you experience true unquestioning faith once, even if only for a moment, you will pursue it again forever.

Thank you for joining me on this journey. Since we are strangers to one another, it seems appropriate to begin with introductions. The most important detail to know about me is that I am an ordinary person – just like you. Until a few months ago, my life was filled to overflowing with the typical triumphs and struggles of a middle-aged woman juggling career responsibilities and motherhood. My little boys had grown into young men, and within a few years they would be finished with college and, with any luck, become self-sufficient. I reassured myself with the hope that the problems of recent years would be resolved by age and maturity, and that our lives would become less rocked by turbulence. Peace beckoned, seeming to linger just beyond the horizon, but it wasn't to be; not in the way I desired it.

In one moment, in just a single instant, all hope disappeared and my life was shattered… forever changed.

Within these pages you will discover renewal and redemption, enduring love, healing compassion, and supernatural power. I did. And my heart's desire is to share it with you so that you may also find comfort in the midst of your pain. I was convinced that I was broken, ruined beyond all hope of repair, and the Lord proved me wrong. He tenderly gathered every jagged piece of my heart and carefully put me back together. The end result was a new person, formed in the image He desired, infused with His power, and infinitely stronger than before.

I readily admit that I am not a seminary-educated Bible scholar. No one knows better than I that there is much left for me to learn about the Lord. My single credential in sharing my story lies in the fact that I am emerging from this tragedy still a walking, talking, functioning human being. The credit for this belongs completely to God. Left to my own devices, you would find me crying and cowering in a dark closet pleading for an end to the torment.

No, on my own, I am nothing special. I am simply a mom who wanted more than anything else in the world for her children to be happy and successful. Perhaps, therein lay the root of the problem. Happiness and success in my mind were defined in worldly terms and standards. But, isn't that true of most families? We all engage to some degree in the pursuit of material possessions that is so encouraged by our society. And superficially, it appeared to be working. My oldest son, Stephen, had some serious problems, as do many teenagers, but we were addressing them. And we loved him so much. I thought that surely our love alone would be enough to help him overcome these issues.

We were living a typical life filled with typical challenges. You could be me.

And then on a December night, my worst fear, the one that always threatened just beyond my consciousness, the one I would never really allow myself to consider, became reality.

What do you do? Where do you turn when the very foundation upon which you have built your world crumbles to dust? Who do you call when you realize that your own strength is ridiculously inadequate to carry you through?

I certainly didn't know, and I was sinking fast. Everything was gone. No hope remained. I had never before experienced such aching emptiness. I desperately needed answers but there were none.

And then, I noticed a faint glow; a glimmer of light flickering at the end of the dark tunnel that had begun to define my world. I didn't expect it. At first, I didn't even recognize it. Yet, even before my puzzled interest could be transformed into complete astonishment, God literally swept me into His loving arms and rescued me.

Are you in need of rescue? Are you also struggling with hopelessness and paralyzing despair? If you are, I understand. Life can become so unbearably difficult that you question whether it is even worth the struggle. For what purpose do we endure such hardship?

You won't find the answers in the secular world. Nothing I had learned in the pursuit of worldly success provided a single ounce of comfort to me when I needed it most desperately.

My answers were born in pain. I discovered some powerful truths during my walk through the valley. When the world offered me nothing, God gave me everything. In times of plenty my heart had remained firmly closed to Him; but once broken, it recognized only its piercing need: a need for Him. During the past year, I have learned to hear, to recognize, and to obey God's voice. Making the decision to take His hand, to close my eyes and to hold on for dear life, has transformed me in ways I would never have dreamed possible.

Is deliverance and redemption also available to you? I believe with all of my heart that it is. You only have to ask. For some, the realization of God comes gradually. Others experience Him flooding their lives in a rush. God knows your need. Regardless of how you meet Him, an intimate relationship with your Savior begins as a budding knowledge that blossoms into full-blown glory within a willing heart.

When I first began to experience God's love surrounding and comforting me, I wasn't completely convinced that He existed. I recognized that something I didn't understand was happening to me, and I began a search for explanations and reassurance. I felt a tremendous need to hear from others who had experienced God in personal and powerful ways, and I craved specifics. I wanted to know, "How did you know it was God? How exactly did He speak to you?" I urgently *needed* to know. Something supernatural was happening to me. I could not deny it and this realization simultaneously comforted and terrified me.

You will come to know me well as I relate the details of our tragedy. I hold nothing back of my weakness, my despair, my doubts, and my fears. Too often, we try to present ourselves to the world as strong and capable. We hide our innermost fears out of a false sense of pride. I have chosen to ignore that natural inclination because I want you to see in me—and my story—your own secret thoughts revealed. I invite you to recognize my undermining, self-defeating emotions as similar to those that plague you.

Measure your struggles against mine. I realize that I am not the only person who has ever suffered devastating loss. Your pain is equally difficult to bear. The reason for sharing my tragedy so openly is not to say that I am unique in my suffering but rather to reveal the extent of my redemption: to contrast my situation in December 2003 with where God has brought me one year later. My emotional condition was critical. It was life-ending. And when I most needed Him, God was huge! He embraced me and shielded me with a love that surpasses description.

As you walk with me along this journey, I encourage you to ask yourself this question, "If God cared enough and was powerful enough to rescue her, will He not do the same thing for me?"

Now it is your turn. Who are you deep down inside where no one else can see? What demons are scratching at your door? Although I don't know your name, there are some things I do know about you. Whether or not you are already a born-again child of God or one not yet convinced of the awesome intensity of His love, you crave answers. You may have sought them in many places you would prefer not to remember; perhaps in the arms of a lover ... in alcohol or drugs ... in overachievement or underachievement ... in the endless pursuit of beauty or the quest for worldly success. You long to know that you are accepted and valued and have a meaning-ful purpose in life. I may not know every need that led you to pick up this book. But of one thing I am absolutely certain: God knows and He cares. You have tremendous value to Him. Your name is written in the palm of His hand and you are never out of His thoughts, not for a moment.

Let me assure you that I also care, immensely. My fervent prayer is for some aspect of my experience to touch you, to change you, and to draw you closer to God. If even the faintest possibility exists that witnessing my struggles and doubts will help you to overcome the same, I willingly lay them bare for you.

As we walk through the birth and strengthening of my faith in our Savior, you will observe that the person with whom you are beginning this journey is not the same person who is with you in the end. The change in my heart was not instantaneous. The develop-ment of faith is a process. My trust, gratitude, and love for God did not spring up overnight. Rather, each grew steadily. I doubted. I wondered. I resisted the concept of obedience. And, thankfully, my Lord isn't finished with me yet. I am undoubtedly a work in progress, and I continue to learn and grow every day. Yet, as I look back at where I have been, the transformation He has made in my heart and in my life is nothing short of amazing.

Let me be clear. I am not proposing my experience as a formula for the way God works in everyone's life or as a standard method in which He communicates. The following account is simply the way He chose to reveal Himself to me. Some of you already have, or will in your lifetime, experience more dramatic manifestations of His power than I have, and others will come to know Him through more subtle means. The end result is the same: a deep, lasting peace; comfort in times of trouble; and the glorious promise of an eternal home with Him in heaven. God, in His infinite wisdom and compassion, provides us with exactly what we need, in exactly the way we need to receive it. Each need is unique, as is each relationship with our Lord.

My life in the past year is described eloquently and succinctly in the words of King David recorded in the 40th Psalm. Although written centuries ago, these verses speak a powerful truth. What solace they have been to me! In my darkest moments, I have whispered them through the tears, repeating them again and again …until I feel His warmth envelop my heart and banish the terror. God's mighty but gentle hand dries my tears and calms the turbulent waters of my soul, offering hope and deliverance from pain. A touch this comforting is available from only one source: God.

What can you do to earn such treasure for yourself? Nothing! It cannot be purchased with good behavior, intellectual ability, or worldly acclaim. Your efforts to save yourself are futile. There is only one path to salvation and freedom. Simply, accept Jesus Christ as your Savior and allow Him to reign as the uncontested Lord of your life. Because of His immeasurable mercy, God will provide the same freedom for you that He did for me. He will raise you from your personal nightmare and miraculously transform your despair into a wellspring of hope and joy.

Don't we all long for that sort of life-altering, rule-breaking, mind-bending miracle? In truth, our battered hearts ache for it.

Despite the stoic face we present to the world, hidden deep behind our smiles and confident exteriors lay a vast emptiness and a hunger that can only be satisfied by God.

Your pain may be of a different sort than mine but its sting is equally as sharp. Regardless of your station in life — man or woman, young or old, businessperson or stay-at-home mom — your heart cries out for a Savior Who has the strength to lift you from your pit of despair.

You haven't faced tragedy yet? I wish I could spare you the pain that is inevitable in every life. You are bound to face loss of some kind: death, rejection, desertion, betrayal, illness, financial loss, disappointment ... the list is endless. Satan has a never-ending and creative supply of tools with which to torment us.

True liberation results from relinquishing control of your life to God. He offers freedom from desperation and worry. I don't intend to suggest that salvation provides you with an impenetrable shield from pain and difficult circumstances. We live in a fallen world. No one is immune from hardship, and no such promise has been made. The difference lies in deliberately laying down your sword and giving the battle to the only One with the power to win it for you.

Aren't you tired? Tired of feeling that you have to manage everything and wondering why you are just not quite good enough to do it?

As a redeemed child of God, you will never again face life's difficulties alone. What an awesome power is contained within that statement. You will always have a devoted friend by your side who is providing you with everything you need to emerge victorious!

At this very moment, you could be one heartbeat away from an event that will knock you to your knees. I pray that you will know what to do while you are down there.

I was in that cold, dark place and our Almighty God joined me there and raised me up. He became my dearest friend and protector.

Won't you allow Him to become yours? Take His hand. He has been reaching for yours since the moment you were born.

What strength do I have, that I should still hope?
What prospects, that I should be patient?
Do I have the strength of stone?
Is my flesh bronze?
Do I have any power to help myself,
now that success has been driven from me?
Job 6:11-13

Chapter 1

The End?

Our journey together begins at a place that looks a lot like the end: the end of hope; the end of a dream; the abrupt severing of a fiercely-bonded and at times volatile relationship; the end of seven years of exhilarating triumphs followed by crushing failures. And for me, this journey begins at the abrupt end of a belief system that had been carefully cultivated for over 40 years.

To strengthen my resolve, I tell myself that these words I am about to write are merely black ink on white paper. They cannot hurt me. Yet that fails to explain why the next lines are so difficult to put onto paper... a spiraling abyss of pain reduced to one sentence:

Late on a cold December night in 2003, just days before Christmas, my twenty-one-year-old son Stephen made the irreversible decision to end his life.

He desired escape. Escape from a pain he could not understand or control. But in that moment, the second it takes to pull a trigger, he also took with him the lives of many who loved him. Not literally and never intentionally. He was the only direct target of the violence that night. However, life as we knew it had ended. Stephen was highly treasured. He left behind a family who loved him madly; a mom and dad with stepparents on both sides; a brother, twenty-one months younger but possessing an emotional connection as close as that of any twin; a step-brother; two step-sisters; and an extremely close, extended family who were devoted to him beyond all reason.

Our unabashedly affectionate firstborn son, he of the blond hair and sparkling blue eyes, the intelligent wit and captivating smile, was gone, and he was not coming back. The world would never know his beautiful spirit: the sensitive and gifted writer, the videographer, and the artist we knew him to be.

Stephen was only fourteen years old when the problems began. Trouble roared into our lives without warning. Like a flood, it sent us spinning out of control and consumed our existence. In retrospect, it seems to have happened overnight. One moment he was a well-behaved honor student with a bright smile and engaging personality, and the next he was transformed into someone we didn't know. His demeanor darkened and he became frequently moody, angry, and unreasonable.

I clearly recall the morning we discovered that Stephen had secrets of which we were unaware. I had first dropped off Stephen at the high school, rushed across town to leave Michael at middle school, and then drove back to my office. I had recently opened my own business, an employment services firm, and there was a mountain of work to be done, so I quickly became immersed in the day's activities. I had only been working for an hour when I looked up from my desk to discover my husband standing in the doorway. I knew instantly by the expression on his face that something was terribly wrong. He asked me to follow him to the car and, once inside, he told me that Stephen was being held at the police station. He had been arrested at school for smoking marijuana in the bathroom.

I was stunned. My first reaction was to deny that it was even possible. There must be some mistake. Stephen was a good kid. He had never been an ounce of trouble. On the short drive downtown, I struggled to accept the truth. When we arrived, the sheriff met us at the door and led us down the stark hallway to his office. As we entered, my eyes immediately searched the room for Stephen. There he sat in an oversized armchair, looking extremely young and scared. His eyes mirrored the stunned disbelief that filled my own.

Only an hour before when I left him at school, he had been considered by all to be an outstanding student. I had never once received a note from a teacher complaining of his conduct. In fact, other parents often praised the behavior of my children. Now, here we sat in the sheriff's office, listening in pained silence as he outlined the possible consequences of Stephen's actions. He was likely facing expulsion from school for the remainder of the spring semester and, not only that, but drug charges as well. His fate would lie in the hands of the Department of Juvenile Justice. We were told that there was a good chance that he could be sent to a jail for youthful offenders. Recently the school district had made a decision to impose stricter penalties on kids who brought drugs to school.

Weeks would pass before we would learn the decision of the school board or of how DJJ would handle his case. Meanwhile, I arranged for counseling with a therapist who was recommended by Stephen's school counselor. I also decided that Stephen would come to work with me every day and assist me with routine tasks around the office. My hope was that in spending so much time together, I could reach beyond the stony mask that had settled upon his face and discover the reasons behind the rapid changes we were witnessing in him. Until the end of the school year, Stephen worked with me every day and we talked continuously. However, I could never break through the wall he was building between us. There was such anger and pain within him, indiscriminate anger that seemed directed towards the world in general.

I attended counseling with Stephen, but I knew in my heart that the sessions were not getting close to the real problem. I expressed my fear to the therapist, my certainty that something vital had changed deep within him. It was evident to me that Stephen's entire attitude about life and other people had changed. Despite her reassurances to the contrary, I was convinced that this issue was far more significant than a teenager testing the boundaries of parental authority. She disagreed and continued to focus her attention on family relationships. Although I could not name the reason why, even back then when everything was just beginning, I felt a gnawing foreboding. Somehow I knew that I had already lost him and that this problem would never be "fixed."

Months passed. Stephen was expelled from school until the new school year began in the fall, and DJJ agreed to place him in a contract program that would allow him to avoid criminal charges as long as he refrained from drug use, continued counseling, and met regularly with a DJJ social worker. We breathed a sigh of relief that we had discovered his experimentation with drugs so early and had a chance to intervene before something even worse could happen.

I told myself that we had been able to turn a dreadful situation into a positive experience. Stephen had learned a difficult lesson, one that could help him to avoid future problems. I tried to convince myself that we were actually fortunate this had happened. That strategy worked until the day I opened one of his dresser drawers and discovered marijuana. It was lying on top on his clothing, not even hidden. My heart sank. I began a thorough search of his room. In addition to the drugs, I found a book about satanic worship and CDs with occult content.

When Stephen returned home, I confronted him with the items I had found, only to have my concern met with contemptuous silence. It was apparent that he did not feel regret for his actions.

The following day, a friend told me about a youth counselor who had appeared on the evening news recently. His name was Archie Morgan and his office was in Anderson, SC, approximately one hour's drive from our home. Archie was a Christian therapist in his early seventies with a passion for helping teenagers struggling with drug abuse and experimenting with the occult. I made an appointment right away, and for several months we visited him weekly.

Archie interacted with Stephen in a straightforward manner that tolerated no excuses or deceit, and Stephen responded to him immediately. They established an easy rapport, and Stephen obviously liked and respected him. This might be the answer, I thought, especially considering how Stephen actually looked forward to seeing him. Slowly, I allowed myself to feel optimistic.

I believed I could detect a slight improvement in Stephen's attitude, and when he returned to school in the fall, we were successful in getting him transferred to a different high school. Here was a chance for a new beginning. I allowed myself to believe that we were making genuine progress, but those hopes were soon dashed. Only a couple of months into the school year, we discovered that Stephen was again using drugs, perhaps even selling them, and had stolen a large sum of money from our home. That was a devastating betrayal.

I called Archie, and within a few days he had Stephen admitted to an inpatient therapy program in Anderson while we worked on making longer term arrangements at a wilderness camp not far from our home. Stephen lived at the wilderness camp from December to May, and we joined him frequently for family counseling. I recall many nights during that time sitting on our patio in the cold and thinking of him shivering in the chilly evening air. I would imagine that he was also staring into the night and looking at the same stars. With a feeling of despair, I wondered what would happen to us. My heart ached for him as my tears fell in the moonlight.

Over the next seven years we tried everything we knew: counselors, a fulltime job, even college and always love. Intermittently, he would do well and hope would bloom in our hearts. When Stephen was on an upward swing, he could charm the birds out of the trees. Almost everyone he met responded well to him. Stephen had a disarming candor in sharing his feelings and a visible vulnerability that drew people to him. But the good times did not last. Our efforts to help him were only temporary obstructions to the self-destructive force within him. That force tore through the barrier of our love for him as though it were nothing more substantial than tissue paper. Now he was gone and we, who would have done anything for him, had failed. The struggles and pain of the past seven years had all been in vain.

Thinking back to his birth and infancy, I could vividly recall an evening when Stephen was only a few weeks old. Several friends had dropped by our home to meet our new son and to wish us well. I had already discovered that change did not sit well with Stephen, and his usual reaction to new people or new surroundings was to emit loud, piercing wails. He took one look at our visitors, opened his mouth, and began to scream. I hurried upstairs with him, laid him on our bed, and lay down beside him to try to calm him while his father entertained our guests. He continued to cry and before long, I joined him. I was young and inexperienced with small children. My mother lived thousands of miles away in South Carolina, and I had no idea what to do to soothe him. I held him close to my heart, and with tears rolling down my cheeks, I made a solemn promise to him. I told him, "Stephen, I am new at being a mom. But I love you with all of my heart, and I vow to become the best mother I can possibly be for you. I will always protect you from harm and I swear that I will do everything in my power to make you happy." I meant those words with all of my being so what had gone wrong?

On December 19, 2003, the call came. I had just returned from Texas with my younger son Michael where he had undergone minor surgery. We arrived home at 5 p.m. and were exhausted. By eleven o'clock that evening, we were sleeping. An hour later, the sharp ringing of the telephone jolted me awake. I answered the call and heard Rick, Stephen's dad, tell me that he was on his way to Stephen's apartment. A detective friend had just notified him that the police had been called to Stephen's apartment by his girlfriend. Stephen was inside, he had a gun, and he had threatened to kill himself.

I woke my husband and dressed quickly, but since Michael was still recovering from surgery, I left him sleeping. We rushed to the car. During the drive over I could not speak. I could barely breathe. A sick feeling of despair and fear threatened to crush my heart.

We arrived within minutes, but as we turned the car into the apartment complex, we were forced to come to an abrupt stop. A police car blocked the road leading to Stephen's apartment. An officer approached and I explained that I was Stephen's mom. The police would not allow us to enter the apartment complex. Instead, we were forced to wait across the street with a deputy and an emergency medical team. In response to our frantic questions, we learned that Stephen had made the suicide threat to his estranged girlfriend over the telephone. The police had arrived within minutes of the call but had been unable to get him to respond since their arrival. He would not come to the door or answer the telephone. Excruciating minutes turned into more than two and a half hours while we waited anxiously, alternately begging the officer for answers and questioning Stephen's girlfriend for details on what had occurred between them.

Helpless and with a feeling of cold dread, we watched as the emergency medical vehicle suddenly raced across the street towards Stephen's apartment. I ran to the patrol car to find out what had happened, and the deputy asked me for Stephen's social security number. Suddenly, I knew.

The officer would not respond to our questions but said that someone would be coming over in a few minutes to talk to us. Paralyzing fear gripped us as we watched a patrol car roll slowly to a stop before us and saw another officer emerge. Our eyes were fastened on him, silently pleading for relief, but the officer's gaze remained fixed on the ground. His words are forever burned into my memory, cutting like a sharp knife through the fog that enshrouded my heart, "I'm sorry. He didn't make it."

Stephen was already gone before the police arrived.

Telephone calls were made to family members. We drove home to awaken Michael and tell him what had happened. By 3 a.m. our family had gathered inside a nearby vacant apartment that the police had made available to us. All of us — his parents, his grandparents, siblings, aunt, uncle, and cousins — stood together, seeking comfort and solace from this horrific nightmare that had invaded our lives. The silence was broken only by sobs and the occasional questions as we tried to piece together the last hours of his life.

I am weeping as I recall those long agonizing hours. I remember asking if I could go to him. I wanted desperately to hold him in my arms and to comfort him, certain that, even now, my love could banish the hurt within him. But the police would not allow us to enter his apartment. They said it was a crime scene. Every agonizing second of that horrific night is burned into my memory. In the months following I have learned to consciously force those images from my mind. To dwell upon them is truly the path to madness.

Was life supposed to continue after this? How could we, who loved and needed him so much, accept his loss? It was inconceivable. Were we really expected to survive?

Without our willing consent or even our participation, one day blended into another and our family stumbled blindly through the next few weeks. There were no visible wounds to reveal our shattered souls to the world, although it seemed as though there should be. Nothing was outwardly visible unless you looked closely into the haunting sadness that had taken permanent residence within our eyes. On the surface, we may have appeared to be doing as well as could be expected under the circumstances. But outward appearances didn't reflect the torment within our souls. Most were not present with us when grief attacked, knocking us to the floor, threatening to destroy our very existence.

Have you also experienced sudden trauma? Overwhelming anguish? A sorrow so intense you could feel it suffocating the life within you? If so, then you are all too familiar with our pain and you understand what others can only imagine. This sort of debilitating grief is not usually visible to others. No, this enemy prefers to attack at night, especially in the dark when we are alone and most vulnerable to assault from the "what ifs." What if we had done this instead of that? Or what if we had said this to him instead of the words that were actually spoken? What if slightly altering one small action or decision would have made the difference and we didn't do it? Such thoughts sent us retreating behind locked doors where we hid our streaming eyes and heaving sobs from the rest of the world, until finally spent, we crawled out and began the cycle of survival all over again.

I truly wanted to give up. The temptation to surrender to the darkness, numb my thoughts and to stay in bed was enormous. But even through my despair, I realized that to give in to that now could quite possibly mean never getting up again. Only by reminding myself of my responsibility to the people who loved and depended upon me was I able to go through the motions of living. Finally, I forced myself to get up, get dressed, and go to work, but I was functioning strictly on automatic pilot, completing only those tasks necessary to keep my business running while my mind was preoccupied with one self-accusing thought after another. I knew that I had done the best I could for him and did not doubt that Stephen was convinced of my love for him. However, my mind seemed viciously intent on clearly identifying and labeling every mistake I had ever made or every decision that may have produced a different result. I was racing headlong into destruction and longing desperately every day for death to take me as well.

Tragedy was no stranger to our family. Ten years previously, I unexpectedly lost my beloved brother Danny in a house fire, a fire that was ignited when he fell asleep smoking a cigarette in bed. Danny and Stephen were remarkably similar, sharing many of the same gifts and personal characteristics, including those that played a significant role in their deaths: depression combined with drug and alcohol abuse.

We had known pain, but we were completely unprepared for the agony of losing our precious son, his life taken by his own hand. People who are deeply and passionately loved by many others don't take their own lives, do they? I didn't understand that depression creates an excruciating loneliness within its victims, even when they are surrounded by loved ones.

Many people are nervous and uncomfortable with the concept of death. Are you? Would you rather discuss practically any other topic? Perhaps you fear the unknown, and the idea of leaving this world terrifies you. Or you may also be grieving the loss of someone dearly loved by you, and the memories are still too painful to confront. Or maybe for you the thought of death is associated with condemnation and punishment from a disappointed and angry God. Whatever the reasons, many people feel that death is a subject better avoided.

You might assume that possessing a genuine belief in God and the knowledge that you will see your loved one again in heaven would automatically translate into an easier acceptance of death. Not necessarily. Despite a conviction that your loved one now dwells in heaven, separation, even when you know it to be temporary, hurts. My arms ache to hold him, to brush the hair from his eyes, to see his smile, to hear his voice, and to feel his warm embrace. My waking nightmare was made even more painful, because in the first couple of months following his death, I wasn't convinced that heaven actually existed. How could I know for sure? Was this the end? Had his death separated us forever?

Death, from whatever cause, provokes powerful emotions of grief and loss. When death is the result of suicide, these emotions are intensified a hundredfold. For family members and friends, the loss of a loved one to suicide adds a sharp edge of guilt to the already piercing sword of grief. The combination can be unbearable. I simply could not fathom why my love or my will was not enough to save my son. I knew that it was not humanly possible for me to love him more intensely or to want his success more passionately. And I was only one of many who felt this way about him. I struggled to make sense of it all. Why had our every effort to save him been futile?

For whatever reason we name and even a few we don't, the apparent finality of death evokes dismay in our souls. God has purposefully embedded deep within us a powerful yearning for eternal life. It is a life that only He can give and one that I came to understand only through Stephen's death. I pray that you will glimpse this everlasting and abundant life as revealed through our tragic experience. I invite you to retrace my journey with me as we approach the spectacular light that called to me through the darkness, and I believe you may even be relieved of some of the fears I just mentioned along the way.

By 2003, in the eyes of the world, I was a successful businesswoman. I owned a profitable company, was a leader on the boards of many civic organizations, and had received recognition and approval from my peers. I was living the American dream except for one critical flaw. Stephen refused to cooperate. He didn't willingly swallow the spirit of competition and the quest for material success that our culture feeds us. Instead of enjoying the material advantages that I worked so hard to provide for him, he challenged me and my beliefs in a seemingly ungrateful way. To Stephen, life was not an exciting, magnificent opportunity. Instead, when he examined the world, he saw only cruelty, selfishness, and greed, and he declared firmly that he wanted no part of it. He used drugs to escape from his disillusionment and retreat within himself. He was bent on self-destruction, and nothing we did to intervene could stop him.

When Stephen died, I saw my world in a different light and abruptly realized the true value of my success and possessions, which was that they had no value at all. Nothing I had acquired was effective in saving my son: our nice home in a well-tended subdivision, our cars, my clothes and jewelry, country club memberships, or any of the expensive items I bought for him. In fact, the advantages our income provided for him contributed to his downfall. The money I gave to Stephen was used to purchase the addiction that stole his judgment and eventually his life. I was forced to question what I had worked so hard to achieve. Of what worth were money and possessions? My son was dead and they were meaningless. Was this the foundation upon which I had built my life? Had I really valued something this superficial when what I truly treasured, my beloved child, lay buried in a cemetery? Not only was my foundation flawed, but I believed that my life had no value as well. In my most humbling responsibility, the one to my child, I had failed miserably.

You might expect that the fears which had haunted me for several years regarding Stephen's safety and wellbeing would have diminished with his death. After all, the dreaded telephone call in the night had come. The terrible words "your son is gone" had been spoken. My worst fears had been realized. It was over.

Not so. Despite all logic to the contrary, I remained tormented by the same motherly concern I had felt since his birth, with three questions constantly swirling through my mind: *Where is Stephen? What is he doing? Is he okay?* These questions assaulted me with an even more alarming intensity than before, if that is possible. Only now, he was gone. I had no way to obtain answers. This was maddening. I could not call him or stop by his apartment to see him and reassure myself that he was okay. I felt driven to find answers to these questions. Not only had I failed by worldly standards, but unquestionably I had failed my children spiritually. My halfhearted attempts to educate them in Christian beliefs were inconsistent and far less than complete. I feared that my deficiency would now have eternal consequences for my child.

Despite the guilt I felt over my own spiritual weakness, I consoled myself with the knowledge that Stephen had been significantly influenced by Christian family members who had faithfully modeled a powerful commitment to God. It wasn't me but my mother who took the children to church when they were little, and it was my Christian grandparents who picked them up from daycare when I was working late. Regardless of the strong bond Stephen shared with them and the impact of their convictions upon his life, I could not be absolutely sure of his salvation.

Just in case the salvation promised by the Christian faith could be true, I frantically searched my memory for indications that he had accepted Christ as his Savior, and I clung to any shred of evidence. I considered the statements he had made about God to me and to others at various points in his life. Although he never told me that he had accepted Christ as his Savior, I knew he had spent a lot of time studying the Bible and seeking answers. I especially wondered at the significance to him of a framed print that hung on the wall of his living room. Clearly out of place amid the pictures of Bob Marley and other musical artists, was displayed a picture of a family gathered around a dining table with heads bowed and eyes reverently closed in prayer. Although every other picture hanging on the walls of his apartment had been shattered the night he left us, this one alone remained untouched. In his distress, he had lashed out with a clenched fist at pictures, light fixtures, and mirrors. Yet, he walked right past this one. It had to be deliberate. Michael shared with us that he had once questioned Stephen about this picture since it seemed incongruous among the others. Stephen replied that he had purchased the print because it gave him a feeling of peace and it made him feel happy. We treasure that picture. Today it hangs in Michael's apartment as a loving reminder of Stephen and of the God who brought him peace.

In addition to the picture, we discovered other puzzling items in his apartment that were inconsistent with his lifestyle. Stored in a file among his important papers, I was surprised to find a church brochure promoting a revival meeting that had been held several months before his death. The topic was the Rapture and the Tribulation. Had he attended? If not, at least I could assume that the subject was weighing on his mind. Surely, I told myself, all of this must mean something.

But I also recalled his telling me once, in response to my suggestion that he seek peace through God, that he had tried that. He said, "I know more about the Bible than most people who are in church every Sunday, and I did everything it said to do and I still feel this way."

In the early days following Stephen's death, the most reassuring and compelling evidence of his salvation came from my mother. She shared with us a conversation she had with Stephen and Michael when they were 10 and 8 years old respectively. The three of them were walking in the woods behind her home, and as she watched them playing and jumping across a narrow gully, her thoughts turned towards the subject of their salvation. She thought of how they were growing into young men, soon to face the stress and temptations of adolescence, and she knew she had to voice her concerns to them.

She called them to her and said, "Boys, I need to ask you something. I know that when I die, I am going to go to heaven and will live there with Jesus, and I want to know for sure that you will be there with me. The only thing you have to do to be there is to tell Jesus you are a sinner and ask Him to save you and forgive you for your sins. Then He will come and live in your heart." She turned to Stephen, "Stephen, have you asked Jesus to come and live in your heart?" He nodded and said, "Yes." "Michael," she asked, "Have you asked Jesus to come and live in your heart?" He also nodded and said, "Yes." She hugged them and they returned to their play, leaving her comforted in the knowledge that their salvation was assured.

When my mother shared this memory with us, Michael recalled it vividly. I felt reassured but still wondered exactly when Stephen had made that decision. Also, I was wrestling with my own uncertainties about God and eternity.

I continued searching, but everywhere I turned I encountered only questions, never answers. And for what was I searching? I wasn't absolutely convinced of the reality of God myself. It appeared unlikely that my questions would be resolved or that my fears would be assuaged. But I knew I could not live like this indefinitely. Something had to change or I was not going to make it. Was there any reason for hope? None that I could see. I resolved to get by as long as I could for my family, and when I couldn't anymore, well, then I just wouldn't.

Unquestionably, the night Stephen left us could have meant the end for all of us. I wasn't the only one engaged in a desperate struggle.

All who loved him were suffering mightily.

God could have left me there, broken and defeated. I certainly didn't deserve any better. Although I had been saved at twelve years old, I had practically ignored Him from that point forward. There was no reason for me to expect Him to care for me. But, in His amazing mercy, He did.

Praise God, He heard my cry and He responded!

O Lord, you have searched me and you know me.
You know when I sit and when I rise;
you perceive my thoughts from afar.
Psalm 139:1-2

Chapter 2

Are You Talking To Me?

As a rebellious teenager, I did not appreciate my Christian upbringing or restrictive parents. Like Stephen, I was convinced that I knew what was best for me and that my parents were obstacles to my freedom and happiness. With the wisdom that comes with age and experience, I now realize that I was extremely blessed. I was raised in a Southern Baptist home surrounded by a loving family who was actively involved in church. My mother was the secretary of our church and performed frequently as part of a gospel-singing group. My stepfather also held leadership positions in our church. With that level of family involvement, any sort of resistance on my part was pointless. In our home it was clearly understood that church attendance was non-negotiable.

So I attended. I accepted Christ as my Savior at twelve years of age following a youth meeting, and I recall feeling very passionate about my new convictions. I committed to reading the entire Bible from start to finish and was soon off to a feverish start. For a while, all was well. Soon, however, I began to skip a day here and there and eventually stopped altogether. I still attended church regularly and actually paid attention most of the time, but somewhere along the way, I forgot something extremely important. Doubt crept in, and I allowed the wonderful feeling of closeness I had experienced with God to fade until I no longer remembered it.

Years passed, and as I grew into an adult with children of my own, I heard others speak of a relationship with God. Quite frankly, I didn't understand it. I was convinced that people are supposed to fend for themselves in this world. In my mind, religion was nothing more than a fantasy that weak people used to feel secure in a crazy, mixed-up world. How can you have a relationship with someone who never communicates directly with you? No one that I knew had ever claimed to see or audibly hear God. From what I could surmise, you were expected to believe in God without ever having any evidence to support His existence. Not me. I was too smart for that. I couldn't, or to put it more accurately, I wouldn't base my life or decisions on something so flimsy. I refused to bend my knee to a God that I could not see with my eyes, hear with my ears, or touch with my hands. I made decisions based on rational arguments, not fairy tales.

I refused to think about God and found myself very uncomfortable on the rare occasions I did attend a church service. I felt like an imposter. Part of this stemmed from knowing that if I accepted the existence and sovereignty of God, I would be forced to alter my behavior. Not that I was doing anything horrible. I was smug in my belief that I was a good person. I was kind to others, friendly to strangers, and tried to live right. I was certainly far better than most.

Additionally, there was the concept of submission to consider. For someone as self-reliant and stubborn as I am, being under God's control was a major obstacle in my mind. I wasn't going to relinquish my life to someone else, not even God. I liked feeling that I was in charge of my own destiny and had no desire to make changes.

Did I ever turn to God during those years? Yes, but only when I encountered great difficulty.

Sound familiar? Does my response remind you of anyone? Possibly, you have found yourself in an identical position.

Trauma strikes and you hit your knees.

Perhaps the words of my prayer will strike a familiar chord in you: "Dear God, remember me? You haven't heard from me lately, but You know I've been a good person. I really, really need for You to fix this problem in my life. If You do this one thing for me, I promise to ..."

Fill in the blank with whatever commitment you have made to Him in the past. We don't hesitate to promise anything and everything when we need His help, do we? What have you promised—to stop gossiping, smoking, or reaching for that occasional drink? Or you may have taken a different tactic, promising to do something for Him as though He needs your cooperation to accomplish His plan for the world. Did you promise to begin tithing, or to attend church every Sunday? Maybe you'll even attend on Sunday nights and Wednesday nights, too!

Yes, we don't hesitate to make Him the God of our desperation.

But what do you do once the problem is resolved? If you are like me, you feel relief that you made it through *somehow* and your promises to God are quickly forgotten. After all, problems just have a way of working themselves out, so why should you feel any obligation?

This time was vastly different for me. I wasn't bargaining with God. I was making no empty promises with the intention of never keeping them. This trauma was too real, and it was not going away. In my pain and shock, it never occurred to me to ask Him for anything. Even if I had, I wouldn't have known what to ask for. God wasn't going to give Stephen back to me, and that was all I wanted. It was all I needed. But I knew that was impossible, so there were no promises to make and no deals to strike with God this time.

So, where was God when my heart was breaking and when I was sinking into desperation?

He reached out to me.

Reflect upon the implications of that image, both for me and for you.

Before I acknowledged Him as sovereign...

Before I had absorbed the full weight of my loss...

Even before my heartfelt cry for mercy, "Help me, if you exist. My soul is dying."

He was there. God knew how desperately I needed Him, and He acted to comfort me.

At first, the signs of His presence were subtle. I didn't even attribute them to God. Although, I have never believed in after-death communications, I began to wonder if Stephen was somehow nearby and attempting to comfort me. Either that or I was experiencing a series of extremely peculiar coincidences.

It began innocently enough. On the day preceding Stephen's funeral I stopped by the funeral home to spend some time alone with him. During the funeral, the pastor would be reading a letter I had written to Stephen, a mother's goodbye to her beloved son, and I wanted to read the words aloud to Stephen privately. Tears fell continuously from my eyes as I leaned over him and smoothed his hair with my fingers. The sight of him lying there so still was heartbreaking. I studied every contour of his face. Even in death, he was beautiful. Finally, I pulled a chair next to him and began to read. In the letter, I referred to the special way Stephen had hugged me. Regardless of how long I held the embrace, he was always the last one to let go. I had just read, "This time, my son, you let go long before I was ready," when I heard the opening notes of Beethoven's "Fur Elise."

The words froze on my lips and I looked sharply at him. Then, with a tremulous smile, I whispered aloud, "Are you talking to me?" I watched transfixed as a tear rolled slowly from the corner of his right eye. This was surreal. Was I dreaming?

Now, I readily concede that the tear I witnessed must have fallen from my eyes as I leaned over him moments before. And, yes, background music was playing the entire time I was there. It had simply gone unnoticed before. The reason for its significance now is that my younger son, Michael, had become quite an accomplished pianist. He was naturally gifted and self-taught. The first piece of music he mastered was "Fur Elise." A few years previously, he had won an award in a talent contest playing this piece, and to our family, "Fur Elise" is firmly associated with Michael.

Coincidence, my mind proclaimed. Yet, even then, my heart told me differently.

I immediately shared the experience with Michael upon returning home, and he expressed regret that he had not accompanied me. Later that evening, we returned to the funeral home for the visitation. We arrived early to allow a few minutes alone with Stephen before friends and other family members came to offer their condolences. As Michael and I entered the room and approached the casket, once again the sweet melody of "Fur Elise" filled the room. Michael turned to me, and our eyes met. I said softly, "This one is for you." We stood together, holding Stephen's hand and weeping, until the song ended.

The next morning began with another unusual coincidence. It was the day of the funeral and I was jolted awake very early by an insistent ringing. The sound wasn't the telephone. I glanced at my alarm clock. It was also silent. The luminous numbers indicated the time was only 6:20 a.m. I sat up and peered into the darkness trying to identify the source of the sound. It seemed to be coming from the direction of my husband's dresser so I awakened him to find it. He discovered that it was the travel alarm clock that was making all of the noise. When he returned to bed, I asked him why he had set that clock and particularly, why so early?

He shook his head and denied setting it at all. He was absolutely certain that he had not touched it. That was certainly unusual. The travel alarm clock was used only on those rare occasions when my husband had a need to arise and shower before me. We could not recall using it for several months. Furthermore, it had never been known to ring without being set in the years before this incident or in all of the months since. There was no logical explanation.

A couple of weeks later, I returned to work to find that a beautiful holly bush covered with bright red berries had been delivered for me. The card revealed that it was a gift from Stephen's physician who, in addition to providing him with medical care, had also become a trusted friend to him in the years that he had treated him. I was seated at my desk writing a thank you card to him when the next unusual event occurred. I had just written the words, "Do you think Stephen really knew how much I loved him?" when I was startled by a tremendous crash. I looked towards my bookcase in surprise to discover that a shelf of books had toppled over causing some ornamental mugs to crash together. The books on that shelf had been sitting there undisturbed for three years. They were purely decorative considering I had never found the time to read them. Moreover, it was unusual that I would be working in this particular office. I seldom spent time here, more frequently working in our accounting office on the opposite side of the building. Wasn't it peculiar that after all this time those books would fall over at the precise moment I happened to be sitting there? Did it have anything to do with what I had just written?

Frankly, I had no idea what to make of it. In my present state of mind, I lacked the ability to contemplate these strange events. It was a tremendous struggle just to get through each day. However, I stored each of them in my heart and resolved to examine them more closely later. *Can these occurrences be mere coincidence? All of them?* I wondered, but I suspected the odds were beginning to get a bit long.

Although it seemed unlikely, I had to ask myself, *Can this be God? Is He talking to me?*

The idea that God might be actively intervening in my life was so far removed from my every day experience that I seriously considered the possibility that I was losing my mind. I struggled with thoughts of self-doubt: *Has grief pushed me over the edge? Am I somehow creating for myself a warm safe haven where I can hide and no longer be hurt?*

Yes, I admitted to myself, *that is definitely possible.*

On the other hand, is it even remotely conceivable that everything I learned about God as a child could be true? That He is real? That He cares about me? What an intriguing thought. Is God tapping me on the shoulder trying to get my attention? And if so, why? I've given Him no reason to care about me.

I came to the conclusion that there were two distinct possibilities here: either I was rapidly going crazy or I was the object of God's attention.

Both options completely unnerved me!

Do you recognize that feeling of turmoil? Are you now or have you ever experienced a time in your life that was dominated by confusion? Where nothing makes sense? If you have ever had to fight to overcome fear, uncertainty, or loss, then this book is written for you. If you long to witness the love and power of God revealed through a specific, personal account, this book is written for you. And if you yearn for a faith that can move mountains, this book is most assuredly written for you.

Our "me-centered" society encourages us to believe that we are the center of our own little world. We measure every circumstance in terms of what effect it will have on us. I admit that I am as guilty of this as anyone. For instance, when facing a trauma or challenge and considering possible solutions, I evaluate alternatives based on the historical success of each under circumstances similar to my own. "Was their solution effective under conditions as severe as those I am enduring?" Without details, I assume not. Wouldn't you agree that in our minds, our own personal problems take on mountainous proportions compared to those experienced by others? If someone facing similar challenges appears to be handling them well or at least better than we are, we automatically assume that their problems are less severe than our own.

In times of personal crisis, we crave a proven solution and, not only that, but tangible assistance in finding it. The most effective problem-solver by far is the Holy Spirit if you are willing to relinquish control and allow Him to draw you into the waiting arms of the Lord.

But suppose you don't know Him? Suppose you are the self-reliant sort who believes no one is better equipped to manage your life than you are. Perhaps hearing the particulars of another's deliverance, someone who suffered under the same delusion, will prompt you to seek yours from the same abundant source.

While I didn't understand what was happening or the meaning behind these strange occurrences, I did feel comforted. Little did I know but God was only just getting started. I had no idea how far He was about to take us.

You have planted much,
but have harvested little.
You eat, but never have enough.
You drink, but never have your fill.
You put on clothes, but are not warm.
You earn wages, only to put them
in a purse with holes in it.
Haggai 1:6

Chapter 3

The Myth of Happily Ever After

W here does it begin, this quest for wealth, recognition, and privilege? As much as I long to rush you headlong into the redeeming truth of Christ and the startling way in which He revealed Himself to me, I realize that I cannot take you further until we first explore the factors that brought us to this point. I include you in that "us" since I suspect that many of you will recognize yourselves to some degree in the many mistakes I have made.

Tragedy was not supposed to happen in my life. I had studied the rules of the world and had learned to play the game well.

Over the years I had incorporated into my belief system the following worldly promises:

"True love conquers all."
"Money does buy happiness."
"Appearance and style are paramount."
"I can accomplish anything I set my mind to."

"Success is defined by money, power, and acceptance."

Where did I learn these principles? It wasn't from my family. My mother never once set me upon her knee and said, "Child, the path to true happiness is found in the pursuit of material possessions." No, the values and lessons taught in my family were directly opposed to these, as were the values I acquired in church and through reading the Bible. So, if I did not begin my life seeking the "fast track to success," what caused me to derail?

The answer is simple: other people. I learned by observing humanity. When I first noticed that the world beyond my front yard was not governed by the principles of my Christian upbringing, I was resistant. However, it wasn't long before my young and impressionable mind became seduced by temptation. The Christian life offered me rules and standards that I felt were difficult, if not downright impossible for me to achieve, whereas embracing the worldly view promised freedom, excitement, and adventure—a much more appetizing meal to swallow. As my fisherman grandfather would say, "I fell for it hook, line, and sinker."

Looking back, I can almost pinpoint the precise moment my values began to shift. I was in the seventh grade. Do you recall the trauma of junior high school? For many of us, few years compare with the misery of that awkward period between childhood and young adulthood. It was here amidst the confusion generated by physical and emotional changes that I first became aware of being measured against new criteria. Not only that, but to my dismay I realized that I didn't measure up very well.

Up to this point my life had revolved around my family, high achievement in school, and playing with my friends. I felt loved, accepted, and confident that I could meet the expectations of the people important in my life.

Almost overnight, that changed. Suddenly acceptance by my peers became essential, and with that acceptance came rigid requirements and new expectations. There were certain shoes and branded clothing that must be worn, social positions to be achieved, and friendships reserved for special people. My family was not wealthy. We did not have the money to spend on designer clothing, dance, gymnastics, or tennis lessons, nor did we belong to expensive social clubs. I felt that I had arrived at the party completely unprepared! So began my separation from my family and their "antiquated" values.

I was a good student of humanity. I observed and I internalized what I saw. What separated the popular and successful from all the rest of us? In my opinion, it didn't appear to be intelligence, compassion, or Christian behavior. In every example I studied, it was money! From my limited perspective, those who had it were happy. I am not saying that at that moment I became consumed with the acquisition of wealth and success. However, the seeds were sown in my heart, and I began to question the teachings of my parents. I decided that my family meant well, bless their hearts, but they were hopelessly out of step with the real world.

I decided that I would be different. Admittedly, I had some catching up to do, but I would learn, and I would be successful. Not only that, but when I grew up and had children, I vowed that they would have everything I had missed as an adolescent. They would never feel the pain of rejection: I would prepare them to compete effectively in this world, and they would always be happy.

This sounds naïve, I know, and as an adult I did not actually sing that mantra aloud. Rather, it became a subconscious conviction that insidiously pervaded my belief system; a conviction born of a message that our materialistic culture delivers to us daily. Radio, television, books, movies: all hype the power of the individual, competition and winning, and the achievement of ideal physical beauty. Consider for a moment the heartbreak and tragedy, the untold misery, violent crime and premature death that have resulted from our inability to measure up.

I thought for a brief moment that I had made it. I was comfortable financially and had a successful career. I enjoyed acceptance and recognition. I shared a deep and abiding love with my husband and my children. Life should have been perfect. I had achieved success and now I was ready to live happily ever after, just like the fairy tale. I had accomplished everything the world told me I needed to, so where was the tranquility and joy? Why did I feel empty?

Stephen probably assessed the situation more accurately than any of us. At the time, he had just entered the ninth grade and was facing the same sort of challenges from which I had vowed to shelter him. "Isn't there supposed to be more than this?" he asked, a query born of hurt and anger. I resented his challenging question more than a little considering how hard I was working to provide him with everything he might want or need. I had no answers for him. Although I didn't tell him at the time, I had often wondered the same thing. Why did each achievement or acquisition bring me only momentary pleasure? Nothing could adequately fill the void within me. No sooner did I finish one project before throwing myself into a new one to absorb my time and energies.

So where was God when I was building my career? I can tell you again where I *thought* He was: nowhere. I was smart. I had built a successful business through my own abilities and hard work. I was in control of my life, and even though there were some problems, I liked being in charge. Admittedly there were times when I would pause and wonder why I had been so lucky – but only to myself. I had never really planned for my career to unfold the way it had. In fact, it seemed to me that success had just happened to me rather than resulting directly from something I had initiated. Despite these private questions, I decided to quietly take the credit and not bother asking "why?" all the time.

So, life continued and became increasingly filled with stress and tension. The situation with Stephen worsened. Arguments ensued.

I share my mistakes with you not because there is anything unique about my story, but rather because there isn't. I am not the only victim of the "happily ever after" myth. We first hear it as children in stories of princes and princesses and their castles. While it may not be the boulder in your life that it has been for me, most of you have encountered it in some form.

Have you ever faced disappointment or rejection in something very important to you and thought to yourself, "If only I had more money, I wouldn't have these problems." You are right. You wouldn't have those problems. But you would have different problems. And problems are problems. They are all uncomfortable.

I didn't realize it then, or I was unwilling to accept it if I did, but there was an answer to Stephen's challenging question about the meaning of life. I understand now that we are meant for something far more significant than the shallow quest for pleasure and comfort. There is no perfect peace or happiness except that found in the love of our Almighty God. You will not find it in wealth, in beauty, or in worldly fame. Money does not solve all problems or bring happiness. How sad for my family that I did not know this then, but I know it now. I learned this lesson in the most difficult way you can imagine.

Sadly, I should have known. I had definitely heard the truth and had many opportunities to believe it. Instead, I rejected the transforming reality of the Lord. Serving God didn't sound exciting, fashionable, or prestigious enough to me, not when embracing worldly priorities made me feel so good about myself. As heart wrenching as it has been, I have confronted and accepted my responsibility for what happened to Stephen. I knew the answers in my mind that could have helped him, and yet I never offered them to him because those truths weren't real in my heart.

Satan delights in reminding me of every failure I made in the hope that I will become paralyzed by guilt and remorse. Instead of succumbing under the weight of that misery, I lay it before God. I have gone to Him on my knees, crying out for forgiveness both from Him and from Stephen. There, kneeling before Him, I find peace, a peace that reminds me I cannot change the past but that I have been forgiven of past sins. God uses my remorse to convict my heart into making sure that I do not miss an opportunity in the future to help someone else with the same questions. That, my friend, is the best use for guilt and remorse.

If you are currently measuring your worth by a financial scorecard as I was doing, you are aching for deliverance. Worldly success is exhausting, but freedom is there for the asking. It involves turning your life over to God.

If you have never accepted Christ as your Savior, you are missing so much – an entire dimension of life that is richer and fuller than you ever dreamed possible. Or perhaps you have accepted God's gift of salvation but remain stubbornly clinging to the belief that you are the best master of your destiny.

What a difference it makes to live free: free from senseless, health destroying worry; free from fear and self defeating recriminations. Freedom is found when you shift your priorities from those valued by this world to those valued beyond this world. And, I assure you, when your sight is firmly fixed on your relationship with God and on pleasing Him, there is truly nothing to fear. All things become possible, not through your own power but through His.

I urge you to accept Him as Lord and Savior. Relinquish control of your life to Him, and ask Him to provide for your needs as you focus on walking more closely with Him. This is the only path to true and lasting treasure.

I ended the last chapter with a description of what many would describe as interesting coincidences, nothing more. Coincidence is defined as chance, luck, or twist of fate. God's Word is filled with examples of the unique methods He uses to communicate with His people. Some were startling encounters; others were characterized by gentle guidance; still others were based on simple faith. God shapes each relationship based upon the needs of each individual and upon the purpose He intends for each of us to accomplish.

Suspend your skepticism for a moment. I understand your doubt and I don't blame you for it. At one time, I also attributed peculiar events to coincidence. Sometimes unexplainable things just happen without rhyme or reason. I told myself that just because we cannot see an obvious cause doesn't mean a peculiar event is evidence of God. I used to believe that, but no longer. God tested this fallacy until I had no reasonable option but to recognize His hand in my life. Now I understand that we are children of providence and that nothing happens by chance. God is in control.

Hallelujah!

O Lord, what is man that you care for him,
the son of man that you think of him?
Man is like a breath;
his days are like a fleeting shadow.
Psalm 144:3-4

Chapter 4

He Knows My Name!

What an amazing revelation! I had spent years warming a church pew, years hearing that Jesus loves me and died for me, and I never truly understood how He could know me personally. Impossible, I thought! There have been too many people that have lived in the past, too many alive now, and too many yet to be born for my mind to grasp that He knows me as an individual.

I could conceive that He loved everybody in general and that "everybody" included me, and I could also accept that Jesus died to save the world and that "the world" included me. However, to imagine that He knows and cares about each person as an individual and that He is concerned about each problem ... well, thinking about that just made my head hurt! I could not comprehend how that was possible.

Has this concept also been an obstacle to your coming to truly know the Lord? Do you honestly, deep in your heart, believe that God knows your name? That He knows where you live and work or go to school? That He knows about the raise you received at work last week, or, perish the thought, that He knows about the post-its you *accidentally* took out of your employer's stockroom and brought home with you yesterday?

If you do, praise the Lord! You have acknowledged His awesome power much more quickly than I, who was forever trying to view Him through the lens of human limitations. But surely there are others like me who, despite everything we are taught, persist in trying to fit the deity of God into a manageable, understandable, and predictable form. I *know* I can't be the only one with these thoughts!

It is our nature. As human beings, this is the method by which we assimilate new information. We learn about our world by observing something new to us and comparing it with what we already know to be true. Then we reach conclusions based upon our stored bank of knowledge. We attempt to make Him human and when that doesn't work, we discount His majesty and power.

In retrospect, I must have thought that when I invited Him into my life as Savior, He showed up for a moment to grant me salvation and then paid attention to me after that only when I did something particularly commendable or horribly bad. I knew I could go to Him in prayer, but I did not feel assured that He heard me, so what was the point? When I did pray, I felt that I was talking to myself or that my prayers were bouncing off of the ceiling. The thought that He would feel sorrow and compassion towards me or that He would be moved to action to help me never occurred to me. If He did exist, He had bigger issues to deal with than me. Who was I that He should be concerned with me?

That covers one obstacle to seeing Jesus as our personal Savior, One who walks with us every moment of every day, but there is another. I touched on it briefly when I mentioned the post-it notes. Does the thought of God knowing your every deed, even your every thought, make you more than a little uncomfortable? Reflect upon your behavior and your thoughts just since you woke up this morning. Some of you are nodding your head, thinking, "I am at ease with that." Others are squirming a little...perhaps a lot.

Could the second obstacle be that there is safety in anonymity? If God isn't watching me, He can't know the mistakes I make or the ugly thoughts that enter my mind.

Friend, I know that He is watching you. How can I know that? Because He revealed to me beyond a shadow of a doubt that He is watching me every minute of every day. And the incredible, earth-shaking wonder of it all is that there is nothing special about me! If He would do what He has done for me, He is longing to do the same for you.

God tells us many times in His Word that if we seek Him with all of our hearts, we will find Him. I fear that often we become caught up in the daily rush of our lives and completely overlook signs of His presence. Open your eyes and your heart to Him. Seek Him!

The next time God called to me was even more unusual than those already mentioned. I didn't know what to make of it, so don't be surprised if you are left puzzled as well.

I first came to realize that God is aware of me as an individual beginning with a situation that involved a unique name. Several years ago, through my business dealings, I came across a name that I had never heard before. I never actually met the individual to whom the name belonged but the name itself caught my attention because it was different. The name was Norbert.

Have you ever encountered anyone named Norbert? I have asked many people since this episode, and no one I have spoken with has ever met anyone named Norbert. Additionally, in the past three years, I have never had occasion to think of him or his name.

One Sunday morning approximately a month after Stephen's death, I awoke first. It was a few minutes before 9 am, and my husband was still sleeping. This in itself was unusual. Jasper would typically arise by 8 am at the latest and leave me sleeping. Not being a morning person, on weekends I generally wandered into the living room around 9:30 or 10:00.

Even more unusual was the manner in which I was awakened. I had been dreaming that the fire inspector was returning to my business to do a follow-up inspection. I saw him approaching the front door from the window of my office and this alarmed me because with everything that had happened in our lives, we had forgotten to replace a burned out bulb in the exit light. My fingers quickly dialed the numbers to call my husband, and when Jasper answered the telephone, I exclaimed, "Norbert is here!"

Suddenly, it was as though the word "Norbert!" was screamed into my ear jolting me awake. My eyes flew open and I felt disoriented. I looked around, realized that I was in my own bed and noted the time. "Norbert, Norbert, Norbert" kept going through my mind, over and over, like a monotonous chant. I arose quietly and went into the kitchen where I prepared a glass of water. Returning to the living room, I turned on the television to a particular channel that frequently shows reruns of *Law and Order*, and doing so reminded me of a day not long ago when Stephen and I had discussed our fondness for this show. Meanwhile, I continued to hear a litany of "Norbert" repeated continuously in my thoughts.

Noticing that the opening credits of a movie were just beginning, I reached for the remote control to change the channel. I paused when a name on the screen caught my eye. It was unusual because the actor only used one name without a last name. When the next name appeared, I almost dropped my water! The actor's first name was Norbert! How peculiar that I would be awakened in such a way and then see the same name on the screen! If the name had been a common one I would have thought nothing of it, but Norbert! The name of the movie was *Ticker*. I read the summary in the TV guide, which said it was a police drama about terrorists who were bombing San Francisco. I saw nothing meaningful or significant in the plot description, so lacking the attention span necessary to focus on a movie, I changed the channel. However, I could not shake the feeling that it was significant. Something bizarre was definitely taking place here.

All other events in my dream were based on an actual situation. The fire inspector was due back to my company any day to re-inspect my business, and we had not yet changed the bulb in the exit light.

I realize how questionable this must sound to you and that you may even be reevaluating your decision to begin reading this book. "Surely," you are thinking, "her strong assertions that God is communicating with her are based on something more substantial than this!" Bear with me. I assure you that they are. I am revealing my story in exactly the way it happened. I had identical doubts at the time.

At this point, I knew only one thing for certain: *someone* was trying to get my attention. God? Stephen? I didn't know, but I was completely intrigued and I wanted to know more!

I would be given the opportunity. I had been provided only the faintest glimpse of how God would use this movie to reach me and other family members. The entire message that He intended would not be revealed for more than a year.

I have told you these things,
so that in me you may have peace.
In this world you will have trouble.
But take heart!
I have overcome the world.
John 16:33

Chapter 5

Dear Lord, It Hurts Too Much!

By mid-February, the shock of losing Stephen was giving way to the unrelenting realization of life without him. I was convinced that Stephen had not doubted my love for him. He had recently told me, "No matter what happens in my life, I always know how much my family loves me." I even felt peace in that I knew I had done everything within my power to save him.

Despite that knowledge, none of those assurances helped to heal my broken heart. Tormenting thoughts continuously reminded me that I would never hold him again. I would never again see that wistful smile, enjoy his clever wit, or answer the telephone to hear his voice say "Hi Moms" on the other end. He added the "s" to the word Mom because he never did anything in an ordinary way. The apparent finality of my loss was more than I could bear.

I recalled how in the few weeks prior to his death, he had begun dropping in on me unexpectedly at work. One of these visits was particularly meaningful. A few days before Thanksgiving, I looked up from my desk to see him enter my door. His expression was serious and I could tell he had a lot on his mind, so I set aside my work and we talked. During this conversation he unexpectedly revealed to me the trauma he felt was responsible for the change in him, the trauma that had robbed him of his innocence as a young teenager. He shared with me how one particular boy in his class had begun teasing him at school. One day this boy had made a big production out of deliberately putting gum in Stephen's hair in front of the student body during an assembly and he described how all the other kids had laughed. While many teachers saw this boy physically mistreat Stephen by hitting him or pushing him into lockers, since the offender was an athlete and quite popular, no one intervened to stop the bullying. This cruelty continued every day for more than two years. Stephen wept bitterly as he told me about the shame of hiding his secret for so many years. He said that he was revealing this to me now because he wanted me to understand there was nothing I could have done.

As I sat quietly listening to my son, a cold rage filled my heart; I resolved to initiate the confrontation with this boy that was long overdue. I would find him. Although he was now twenty-one years old, I felt that he needed to face the damage that his behavior had inflicted on our entire family. At the same time, I was also encouraged that Stephen was sharing the secret he had kept locked within him. I was convinced that this was the first step in healing. Now that we knew the enemy, I reasoned, we could confront the problem and deal with it. But it wasn't the beginning of healing. It was the beginning of the end. It was Stephen's first step in saying goodbye.

During the first month following Stephen's death, my thoughts frequently turned to this young man, so that consequently, in addition to the feelings of pain and loss I was already struggling with, I now dealt with guilt, anger, and thoughts of revenge. I blamed him with a vengeance and wanted desperately to hunt him down and force him to acknowledge the damage he had done. I wondered what I would do if I stood face to face with him. It was easy to imagine that situation escalating very quickly beyond my control, so I waited. Someday he would be held accountable for the damage he caused.

I returned to work, and for a few days at a time I would tell myself that I was doing okay. Grief was always lurking behind me, though, menacing and threatening. I began to think of it as a dark cloud, a palpable presence that I could sense creeping up behind me intent on my destruction. I feared that if I turned quickly enough, I would actually see it.

At times, grief did consume me. There was one evening in particular, February 11, 2004, less than two months after Stephen's death, when I felt I was drowning in the deepest pit of despair. I began crying uncontrollably in the car during the short drive home from work. Later that evening, my longing for Stephen drove me upstairs to the room where I had placed all of his belongings. I sat there on the bed looking intently at his photographs on the wall and at the paintings he had created, searching for hidden meaning in his expression or within the subject he had chosen to paint. And I sobbed. My anguish led me to the closet where I pressed my cheek against his wool coat. Breathing in deeply, I tried to absorb his scent, his being. With my eyes tightly closed, I could almost feel his thin shoulders inside.

Distraught and angry, I returned to the bed and literally trembling with emotion cried out to God, "How could You give me such love for a child and then allow him to be torn from me like this? Do You hear me? Do You know that I am dying inside? If You are there, I need to hear from You. I have to know that my child is okay and that he is with You, or else I just cannot go on."

I realized that if this pain resembled in any way the misery Stephen experienced as a result of his depression, then I could understand his decision to die. No one can hurt like this and live. More than an hour passed unnoticed as I cried and begged God to end my suffering. Finally, exhausted and spent from sobbing, I knelt by the bed and prayed, "God, I am not going to make any ridiculous promises like I have done in the past. I am simply begging for Your mercy. I need a message from You, and not something obscure that I must interpret like the "Norbert" thing. I desperately need a sign directly related to Stephen that I will recognize immediately as Your answer to my prayer."

As I returned downstairs, I noticed that my husband had fallen asleep on the sofa. I decided to calm myself by reading in bed for a few moments before trying to sleep, so I placed my book on the nightstand and walked to the head of the bed to turn down the covers. In doing so, I pulled them up too far from the bottom, prompting me to walk to the foot of the bed to straighten them.

I lifted the bottom of the bedspread and began to pull but stopped abruptly at the sight of the object lying on the floor. There at my feet just under the corner of the bed was a single penny. You may not see anything significant about finding a penny on the floor. After all, it is hardly uncommon for people to drop coins. It was only a penny. However, I knew without being able to explain why that it was extremely important. I recalled how my beloved Grandfather, Pop, would delight in finding pennies. He said that they were gifts from God, and in the three years since Pop had left us to go to heaven, my family had discovered pennies in some peculiar places, even on his grave. Stephen adored my Grandfather and had been very close to him.

All of these things crossed my mind as I stood there, staring at the penny and barely daring to breathe. It was lying facedown. I raised my eyes towards heaven and said slowly, "God, that isn't good enough. That penny could be lying there for many reasons. The only way I will believe beyond all doubt that you placed it there for me and that Stephen is with you is if that penny is dated the year he was born."

Slowly, I knelt to pick it up. My trembling fingers turned it over and I almost strangled on my tears. Only this time, they were tears of joy! The penny was stamped with the year 1982, the year Stephen was born! Was I sure? What if I misread it? It was several long minutes before the tears stopped flowing faster than I could wipe them away, enabling me to double-check the date. It was truly there: 1982! I fell to my knees crying, "Thank you, God! Oh, Thank you God!" The agony in my heart dissolved to be replaced by jubilation!

In that moment God literally put my son back into my arms. Although I could not see Stephen now, I had the promise that one day I would hold him again. I would see his sweet smile and talk with him again. That was enough for me!

I hope, on that glorious day, that God will understand when I am unwilling to let him out of my sight for a few thousand years! One day, if you are a born-again child of God, you will also be reunited with your loved ones who are Christians. Can you imagine that celebration?!?

My thoughts turned to the knit cap that Stephen had worn to our family gathering on Thanksgiving. He had just purchased it the day before and was quite proud of it. After finding it in his apartment I had placed it in one of the drawers of my dresser to keep it close to me. Now, I retrieved it and lay down upon the bed with the soft wool pressed to my cheek. I fell asleep with it in my hand and have slept with it under my pillow every night that I have been home since that amazing night. It is a reminder of my promise from God. I slept deeply that night, and when I awoke the next day, I was filled with a joy and peace that sent my spirit soaring.

It occurs to me that someone reading this book may believe that I was wrong to test God. I don't see it that way. I begged God for something that my soul needed to survive, and He gave it to me! My plea was not intended as a demand for God to prove Himself to me. It was a heartfelt cry of desperation.

Consider for a moment what this meant to me:

Stephen is alive and in heaven!

I will be with him again!

God is real! And He cares!

He knows me! And if He knows me, He knows you as well!

Everything I have been taught about God is true!

I was literally floating on a cloud for several days. I took the penny to a frame shop and had it mounted and framed. Since Michael was expected home from college for the weekend, I decided to give it to him to serve as a source of comfort. He would be arriving late in the evening after I had gone to bed so I left the framed penny on the nightstand in his room along with a short note.

The following morning Michael thanked me, and then he curiously asked if I had selected a penny dated the year he was born and placed it beside the framed penny. I had not. But it was there.

We marveled at what was happening to us.

Then Satan attacked.

Unbidden and unwelcome thoughts assailed my mind: *Just a coincidence. Do you know how many thousands of pennies were minted that year? It isn't so remarkable that a penny would be lying there with that date on it. How do you know it was God? You just turned this into what you wanted it to be. Or if you won't accept that, suppose God is tricking you to get you to serve Him the rest of your life? When you get to heaven, Stephen won't be there. Or maybe God is just using this to comfort you and He figures that once you are in heaven, you will understand that He lied to you for your own good.*

I felt viciously attacked and robbed of my peace to some degree. Not completely, but now I had doubts … big ones. Perhaps you are even thinking some of the same things as you read this. Well, my friend, in the words of our precious Savior to Nathaniel in John 1:50, "you shall see greater things than that."

I didn't know it then, but God wasn't going to leave me (or you!) swimming in doubt. He had much bigger and bolder things planned. But before we travel further, let's take stock of where we are now.

I was beginning to understand the compassion of God, but I still had not accepted the deity of God. I loved Him but did not completely trust Him and was not yet willing to serve Him. In other words, I was thoroughly grateful for the revelation He had given to me, but I wasn't ready to relinquish control of my life to Him.

Without intending disrespect, I described my feelings to my mother in this way: "I love God and cannot wait to see Him when I get to heaven, but I hope He understands that if Stephen is standing behind Him, I will run right past Him to get to Stephen, and then we will thank Him together. I want to see my son!"

I hang my head as I write these words. Do you see how little I deserved God's mercy and compassion? Knowing Him as I do now, I am ashamed that I entertained thoughts such as these even for an instant. I reveal this to you because as you draw closer to God, Satan will attack from every angle he can. If you persist in turning your thoughts to God despite Satan's distractions, that evil one will attempt to distort your thinking. I don't want you to feel that you are the only one who has experienced ungrateful thoughts such as these.

My mom merely smiled in her understanding way. She didn't react in horror or in judgment. Rather, she added a critical detail to my musings of a reunion in heaven. As I have grown in understanding, I came to realize the profound truth of her words. She told me, "Debbie, Jesus loves you so much that when you close your eyes and breathe your last, He will meet you holding Stephen out to you." Am I not absurdly and undeservingly blessed to have such a wise woman for my mother?

I don't know about you, but I need that kind of love and understanding both from God and from my mom. What an amazing Lord!

For I am convinced that neither death nor life,
neither angels nor demons,
neither the present nor the future,
nor any powers,
neither height nor depth,
nor anything else in all creation,
will be able to separate us from the love of God
that is in Christ Jesus our Lord.
Romans 8:38-39

Chapter 6

Oh, Mighty God

D o you believe in miracles? I didn't. Where are the amazing
events like those described in the Bible? I wanted to know.
The parting of the Red Sea; the transfiguration of Jesus; all of us
could get behind a God like that, couldn't we? We never hear of this
sort of thing today. Does that mean miracles no longer happen?
Perhaps the fault lies with us. We are no longer looking or listening.

Consider this: suppose someone claimed to walk through the
middle of a sea on dry land. If there were no television cameras to
record it, would you believe it?

Surely God must become impatient with our closed minds and
hardened hearts. What if I had listened to Satan's hateful voice in
my ear rather than opening my heart to God bit by bit? Would God
have stopped trying to reach me? I don't know. I hope not. If my
growth and maturity in Christ depended only upon my alertness and
attention to the details around me, I would be in deep trouble. All

who know me well will tell you that I am usually oblivious to the small details in life. I prefer to think of it as simply focusing on the bigger picture.

The point I am making is this: God may be speaking to you just as He has spoken to me, and you may not be listening. Do you look for Him? Do you seek evidence of His hand in the circumstances of your life?

Or, instead, do you pause for just a moment in awe at a startling coincidence and ask "Could it be?" but then shrug it off because you defer to the "voice of reason" which tells you that life is filled with random coincidences? When you learn of an event that appears supernatural, do you automatically reject it as a hoax? Admittedly, there are some people willing to perpetuate a lie for financial gain. But what if there is no financial gain involved, such as in my case, and what if it really is God trying to speak to you through circumstances that He has orchestrated?

How I struggled with this. I could think of many farfetched, but natural explanations for seemingly unnatural phenomena. Just because an event appeared to be supernatural didn't mean it had to be God, did it? The people who believe those fairy tales are just gullible, right? They must be weak and in need of something or someone more powerful than themselves in which to find strength.

Take a break for a moment and prepare a glass of tea while I give myself a sound beating! I can't imagine why God cares enough to put up with me.

Why is it that when our most brilliant scientists are still struggling to unravel all of the mysteries contained in the workings of a single cell, we persist in our reliance on human reasoning?

Why are we so blind to the truth before us? God created the world and everything in it. There are no boundaries He cannot overcome. He created the laws of physics and He can defy them anytime He wishes. We don't have to understand how miracles occur for them to be true. Truth persists despite our disbelief!

For instance, what is a dream? Is it simply an internal process of your mind that combines reality and fantasy in a series of images while you are sleeping? Most of the time, this is probably true. Yet, could dreaming sometimes be used by God to share with you important truths? He has been known to use dreams to communicate before!

Over the next few weeks, several of Stephen's close relatives were blessed with vivid dreams in which he visited with them and hugged them. His brother, Michael, both of his stepsisters and his aunt dreamed of spending time with him and of being reassured that he was alright. Each was deeply moved by the encounter and described their dream as feeling exceedingly real, including the physical sensation of touching him. I relished their accounts but longed for such an experience myself.

The events of the past few months had ignited a compelling hunger within my heart to learn more about this God who cared enough to reach out to me. I immersed myself in Christian books and music and began reading the New Testament. I expected this to be merely a review since I'd had many years of exposure to the Bible from my Christian upbringing. I'd heard all the Bible stories before. However, I quickly discovered that I knew absolutely nothing. I no longer read as a child but rather as an adult with a lifetime of experience. Now I read to quench a thirst, seeking understanding and application to my life. Everything was brand new. The Word of God ministered to my soul and revealed to me that God had expectations of me. And even better than that, I found assurance that He would give me all I needed to meet those expectations.

Christian music also touched me deeply, reaching the hurt places within my heart and comforting my wounded spirit. I purchased several WOW CDs because they contain a wide selection of Christian performers, and I was unfamiliar with individual artists or groups. Just a few days after my purchase, God granted me a moment with Stephen that involved one of the songs I had heard for the first time on a WOW CD.

My dream occurred on the evening of April 6, 2004. Stephen was a little boy again and appeared to be approximately seven years old. He was playing with Michael at my mother's house. I immediately noticed the expression on his face. His blue eyes sparkled and were literally dancing with joy. Although Stephen had been a happy child, I had never seen him like this. I stood silently nearby, watching him as he played and laughed with Michael. I realized that he was dead and it made me sad. Suddenly, he looked up and smiled at me. Then he reached out his arms to me. As I knelt to hug him, I thought to myself, *I am going to get to hug him, to touch him!* and joy flooded my heart. I pulled him into my arms and held him as though I never planned to let him go. I could literally feel his small body pressed against me.

I awakened abruptly, but I could still feel the sensation of him in my arms and the weight of his arms around my neck. I became aware of a melody that seemed to be playing within my mind. The song was from one of my new CDs, and I had only listened to it once or twice. It is titled, "Better Is One Day."

The lyrics of the chorus, in case you are unfamiliar with the song, are as follows:

> Better is one day in Your courts
> Better is one day in Your house
> Better is one day in Your courts
> than thousands elsewhere.

The chorus repeated over and over. I noticed that the time was 5 am. I thought to myself, *Even though Stephen has to answer to God for how he spent his life, he is telling me that one day in heaven is vastly better than anywhere else. He is happy.* I felt tremendous reassurance and fell into a dreamless sleep. When I awakened a couple of hours later, I could not recall the exact words, only the general theme of the song.

Was this merely an attempt by my subconscious mind to obtain comfort by telling me I had received a message from God? I suggest that you suspend judgment until you have read the next page!

On a scale of one to ten, with ten being fully believing and relinquishing control of my life to God, my belief meter at this point was around a seven.

On May 12, God did something that blew "ten" right off the scale!

May 12th is my brother's birthday. I mentioned previously the strong family resemblance between my brother Danny and Stephen and that both suffered during their short lives with substance abuse and depression. Stephen was greatly affected when Danny died at the age of 28.

In remembrance of Danny, my sister Dee and I generally take my mother to lunch on his birthday. This date was also significant to us because it was the date three years ago that my grandfather, Pop, died peacefully in his sleep.

On Thursday, May 6, five nights before we met for lunch, I experienced a dream that was vastly different from any I have known before. When it began, I was standing outdoors. Unexpectedly, my grandfather appeared approximately ten feet in front of me. Since Pop went to be with the Lord, I have had many dreams of him and have always awakened crying real tears. Yet, I have never experienced anything to compare with this.

Words are completely inadequate to describe the intensity of the joy and happiness that flooded his face. He actually radiated light. As I stood frozen in place, awed by the glow that surrounded him, I became overcome with a deep fear. When he spoke, my fright dissolved and I felt shame that I had felt momentary fear of someone I loved so dearly.

Pop ignored my reaction and told me that he was aware that my grandmother had been worrying about money recently. However, she had access to some money that she had forgotten about, and he wanted me to get it and give it to her.

I eagerly agreed to help, and in my dream he showed me where to find the money in the house they'd lived in for almost twenty years. He instructed me to lean down to my left and reach low, approximately one foot above the floor, and slip my hand in between a stack of some sort of fabric. There I found a bag that contained the money.

When I held the bag in my hand, he told me to take it to Granny. He emphasized that it was very important that I give her a message. I was to repeat it to her precisely.

Immediately after he revealed the message, I woke up. It was still the middle of the night and I lay there reviewing the dream in my mind and trying to absorb what had just occurred. I knew this was no ordinary dream. I was convinced that something very significant had happened to me. I recalled the dream in great detail but puzzled over the important message I was told to deliver. The message was, "The moose is loose."

What a disappointment. Every nerve ending in my body was screaming that something amazing had occurred yet this was the critical message! Was this a joke? We don't even have moose in South Carolina!

I couldn't make any sense of it. Should I tell anyone? Who would take me seriously with a message like that? I decided not to say anything right away but could not get it out of my mind. I thought of it continuously, especially of the light that radiated from Pop and my surprising fear of him. I felt deeply disturbed and ashamed that I had reacted in fear of my dear grandfather. I love him! I had never before experienced fear of him, but I had to admit that I had never witnessed him glowing before either!

On May 12, I met my mother for lunch. Shortly after I arrived, she casually asked if she had told me about the strange incident involving Pop's moneybag.

I looked at her sharply and managed to say, "No... what are you talking about?"

One of Pop's longtime hobbies was coin collecting. She explained that something very peculiar had happened that weekend involving Pop's coin collection. A few months before his death three years ago, Pop had given his coin collection to his three daughters, and my Aunt Bobbie had taken it to her home in Augusta where she hid it for safekeeping.

On Friday, the day after my dream involving Pop and a bag of money, Bobbie's son, Chris, was visiting her and spent the night at her house. Throughout the evening, they were in and out of his room and noticed nothing unusual. The following morning Chris entered the kitchen holding a bag and said "Mom, what is this?" Bobbie responded that she did not know and asked where he found it. He replied that when he got out of bed, he discovered it lying in the middle of the floor at the foot of his bed.

They opened the bag and were astonished to realize that it was the bag that contained Pop's coin collection. Puzzled, Bobbie rushed to the laundry room where she had hidden it many months before. Desiring a safe place for it, she had wrapped the bag inside of a sheet and had hidden it between some old linens. The sheet now lay unwrapped and tossed haphazardly over the stack of linens. The bag containing the coin collection had mysteriously made its way during the night to Chris's room.

They were alarmed. Had someone been in the house while they were sleeping? She and Chris awakened her husband and they searched the house for signs of an intruder. They could find nothing. No one other than Bobbie even knew where the coin collection was hidden. I did not even know it existed!

As my Mother revealed this story to me, I could barely contain my excitement! Once she reached the end of the tale, I said, "Mom, I don't know what this means, but I have something to tell you." I described my dream to her and we marveled over the similarities in the two events. Obviously there was some correlation between my dream and the traveling moneybag at Bobbie's.

She asked me to describe the bag of money in my dream. I used my hands to demonstrate the height and width and stated that the bag was either green or blue and that it had a zippered top. She was incredulous. "Debbie, the coin collection is in a green vinyl bank bag with a zippered top!" I then told my mom about the odd message I was supposed to relay of "the moose is loose." We both shook our heads in puzzlement over that one.

Later on, my mom called Bobbie and asked her to describe the exact location within the closet where the bag had been hidden. Amazingly enough, the collection had been located on a low shelf approximately the same height from the floor as it had been positioned in my dream. The soft fabric in my dream would have been the stack of linens in her closet! How could this be possible?

And what did the odd message mean? Why was it important?

Later that evening while watching television, I began to feel strongly that I should read the Bible. Stubbornly, I decided that I would rather research an unrelated topic on the Internet. Yet, I could not shake the feeling that I was supposed to read the Bible. I resisted. Following my initial inclination, I pressed the power button on the computer and positioned myself comfortably in front of the monitor all the while arguing with myself about reading the Bible. I watched the screen while it booted up and began the connection to the MSN homepage. Just as the familiar page came into view, the process was abruptly interrupted by an error message informing me that the system had encountered a fatal error and Windows was shutting down. In exasperation, I conceded defeat and picked up my Bible. Obviously, it was pointless to continue in my rebellion.

Unsure where to start, I allowed the pages to fall open randomly and began reading in Genesis. Interestingly enough, the passage relayed the story of Joseph and the role that dreams played in his work for the Lord. How fascinating that the subject matter just happened to be about dreams, I thought. I read the chapter with great interest and decided to try the same method again. This time the pages opened to Daniel, chapter 4, which depicts how Daniel interpreted the dreams of Nebuchadnezzar and how his ability to do so ideally positioned him to serve the Lord.

This must mean something! I considered calling my mother to tell her what had happened but decided that 10:15 p.m. was too late to call.

Within seconds of that decision, my telephone rang. It was my mother. She called to tell me that Bobbie had spent the evening on the Internet trying to solve the mystery of "the moose is loose" and had discovered something amazing! It seems that among serious coin collectors, the word "moose" is used to signify an exceptionally valuable coin! This was confirmed on several different websites. Additionally, Bobbie pointed out that within the bag was a handwritten list my grandmother had made of the contents. The list was arranged in two columns. One was titled "sets." The other was titled "loose!"

What an incredible demonstration of God's power and the lengths to which He will go in order to achieve His purpose! If I was having difficulty accepting the deity of God before, that obstacle to my faith had been permanently removed! The day that God began physically moving objects around in my life and placing corresponding dreams in my mind to get my attention, trust me, dear friend, I began listening!

Since that evening, I have felt strongly that God was revealing Himself to me to prepare me for a specific purpose. I am convinced that every significant event that has occurred in my life, both the good and the bad, has been designed to shape me into someone who could be used by Him. Ephesians 2:10 tells us, "For we are God's workmanship, created in Christ Jesus to do good works, which God prepared in advance for us to do."

While the events in my life were not of my choosing and left me reeling, they were never a surprise to God. I felt as though the Lord had walked into my life with His hands outstretched, offering me the opportunity to rise above my misery and participate with Him in turning tragedy into glory. My response was immediate: Count me in!

What about you? The same offer He made to me is extended to you. Are you truly content with where you are in life? Is your heart filled with a sense of satisfaction and clear purpose? It can be. The choice is yours. It is as simple as taking His hand.

My prayer is not that you
take them out of the world
but that you protect them
from the evil one.
They are not of the world,
even as I am not of it.
John 17:15-16

Chapter 7

A New World?

When I was seventeen years old, I left the home in South Carolina that I had known for most of my life and moved to a small town in northern Minnesota. It was a spur of the moment decision. My father lived there along with my stepmother and half-sisters, and since I had not had any contact with him in seven years, I felt a need to reestablish a relationship with him. Also, the thought of starting over somewhere far away appealed to my adventurous spirit.

At the time, I lacked purpose in my life and realized that to continue on my present path would prove detrimental to my future. Recognizing the need for change, with barely a moment's hesitation, I placed a telephone call to my paternal grandmother and told her of my desire to complete my senior year of high school up north. She wired the money for airfare, and the next day I boarded a plane to begin my new life!

In an act of impulsiveness typical of youth and inexperience, I failed to gather any details about the town that would become my home for the next three years. It wasn't Greenwood, I reasoned, so that was good enough! You know that old saying, "the grass is always greener?" Imagine my surprise when I arrived at my destination to discover that the entire population of the town hovered just under 500. The nearest city, Grand Rapids, was located twenty minutes away and was only one-third of the size of my hometown in South Carolina!

Furthermore, my southern upbringing had done little to prepare me for life in the northern wilderness. In Minnesota, hunting and fishing are apparently pastimes enjoyed by all, men and women alike. All, that is, except me! I was completely out of my element. At seventeen, I could not have felt more out of place if I had been picked up from the earth and set back down on Mars! Where was the mall ... the restaurants ... the cute clothes? Everyone was so bundled up here. And the cold! I thought I had experienced cold before, but it didn't take long for me to realize that I didn't even know the meaning of the word. And everyone talked funny. Or more accurately, I should say that to them I sounded peculiar. I was an oddity.

Have you ever found yourself in a similar situation? Perhaps it was a move to a new town, or the first day at a new school or a new job, or some other major life change. Remember the initial awkwardness; the sense of loss; the feeling that everything familiar and comfortable has disappeared? A few individuals thrive in that environment, but for most of us, change is difficult, even when it is a positive change.

In time, I learned to adapt to my new surroundings and developed a strong appreciation for the people who lived there and for the natural beauty of the area. It was simply different at first, and different can translate into unnerving. While I never did develop a desire to hunt or fish, I did manage to find a place for myself in an environment that was strange to me.

Sometimes we avoid new experiences, even those that could be enormously beneficial to us, simply because we fear change. Even if we are unhappy where we are, staying there is familiar. We know our role and what is expected of us. To an unbeliever, the idea of becoming a Christian might be intimidating, even frightening. Satan uses that fear to his advantage. He is adept at identifying our weaknesses and then capitalizing on them. He is the master of doubt, flooding our minds with misconceptions: *Christians are holier-than-thou, boring people, aren't they? What would I be forced to give up in order to follow Jesus? And Christians are so good, or at least they pretend to be! I know I can't be perfect, so why even try? That just isn't me.*

What sort of myths does Satan weave to keep you in bondage? Has he ever whispered these lies to you? *You'll lose your freedom; your personality; your friends; your hobbies. You'll lose every-thing that you enjoy. Check your independent will at the door! And by the way, you may as well resign yourself to tiptoeing through eggshells for the rest of your life in an effort to deny your basic human nature and avoid punishment from an angry God.* Yes, Satan is very skilled at knowing just the lies that fit perfectly with our weak human nature.

I believed those lies. If you have fallen prey to the same, you are definitely not the only one. Many have allowed Satan's deception to rob them of the full, abundant life we are promised by God.

Pushing beyond those doubts and stepping into the light requires faith and an intense longing for something that you may be unable to define. You just know there has to be more than this! God placed that longing in our hearts. We search the world for that one elusive something, that connection that will finally make us feel whole and complete. We find it only when we turn to Him.

Does salvation result in captivity? Absolutely not! Experiencing the reality of an intimate relationship with God means freedom from bondage, forgiveness from every sin (regardless of how heinous), and a love and acceptance that will envelop your heart in an eternal embrace. In a word, it is glorious! But does it involve change? Oh yes.

Are you tired of feeling that your life is without meaning? God has a purpose for you!

Have you been hurt by faithlessness and betrayal? God will never leave you or reject you!

Are you suffering from insecurity or low self-esteem? You were intentionally and wonderfully created by God Himself!

Change? Yes, please. We are dying for it!

Could this description fit your life? You have sought happiness everywhere but could find it nowhere. One day you finally accept that you cannot do it on your own and wonder about that persistent tugging you have felt upon your heart. *Could God really be the answer to what I am missing?* you ask yourself. You open the door of your heart just a little at first, then a little bit more. Finally, realizing that your own methods have brought only heartache and emptiness, you fling it wide open to the realization that you need Him. You repent and invite Christ into your heart.

The choice is so easy. Yet the ramifications of that moment extend into eternity.

What a difference a single decision can make.

You are indeed changed. For one thing, the Holy Spirit now abides within you, filling and molding your heart. You will never again walk alone.

For another, you are heaven-bound and are no longer "of this world."

What does that mean? How does it feel? How does your life change in response to it?

I considered avoiding this topic. To be honest, I felt uncomfortable exposing so many of my private doubts and fears to public scrutiny. But God would have none of it. For this journey to be of real value, we must take a look at what you might expect to happen to you after accepting salvation or rededicating your life to God.

Surely, life becomes problem-free from this point forward. No more illness, pain, or everyday hassles of life. That stuff is long gone! I am a born-again child of God, and inherent within that is a shield of protection from hardship. Bring it on! As long as I do what God wants me to, I can expect peace, joy and happiness all the time. I am so ready!

Yes, you will experience such glory. God's Word tells us in 1 Corinthians 2:9, "However, as it is written: No eye has seen, no ear has heard, no mind has conceived what God has prepared for those who love him." But that promise will be fulfilled in heaven, not earth.

Satan has permanently lost his claim to your soul, but he is not finished with you yet. His mission now becomes to attack your faith.

Your life on earth will continue to be fraught with dangers and pitfalls. Satan views these attacks as his opportunity to immobilize you so you will never become a threat to him. I have learned to think of them as *opportunities for growth*. Actually, it is usually in retrospect that I think of my own challenges in such glowing terms. It isn't always easy to find the gift within the suffering at the time you are caught in its painful grip. Regrettably, with some Christians, Satan is successful in his mission.

A new Christian often feels a tremendous hunger for God but lacks the experience to know how to withstand such an onslaught from Satan. Sometimes the most debilitating problems of our lives occur just after salvation or a renewal of faith. Additionally, you may experience doubts and a loss of confidence just when you need strength the most.

Part of the problem is that you now feel as though you are walking in a strange land. Actually, the world is the same but you are different. You have not yet replaced your old habits or ways of thinking with new ones. Your former methods of handling adversity are ineffective, but you fall back on them at first. You aren't accustomed to having a trusted Friend right by your side willing to guide you and direct your path. You may not immediately look to God for a solution or for help in managing your indecision, fear, anger, or pain.

Ideally, salvation would automatically instill in your conscious mind everything you need to know to become a fully functioning disciple of Christ. Instead, it is a process. Unless you allow Satan to impede God's plan, you next enter a period of growth and maturing where you will develop effective defenses. Prayer and scripture are vital learning tools and will be important in revealing God's will for your life.

When I accepted God's invitation and agreed to follow wherever He chose to lead me, I felt that I had entered a new land. The landscape was familiar. My home, my business, my town all looked the same, yet everything felt completely different.

In simple terms, my focus had shifted. Instead of becoming undone by the challenges of everyday life, my sights were now firmly fixed beyond this horizon. Petty issues that would normally try my patience became inconsequential. No longer were my days measured by how much work I accomplished or by my company's growth on a sales report. Instead I began to measure their value by how many opportunities arose for me to share with others the amazing difference Christ was making in my life.

A good day for me meant that I had an opportunity to share with others what I had learned. By their response, I could see that hearing of my experience strengthened their faith, and I felt amazed that God would use me to help someone else! Each sharing experience lifted me a little further out of my pit, and I began to long for more.

Although I was excited, I was also frightened, but not because I feared rejection. That was not a factor at all. In some ways, extreme suffering in itself is liberating in that it completely obliterates the fear of what others will think of you. Additionally, I had discovered an amazing truth that changed my life and to keep it to myself was inconceivable. I would burst! Rather, my fear was that I did not know enough. What if someone asked me biblical questions and I did not know the correct answers? I was new to this and inexperienced; I feared saying the wrong thing and becoming a hindrance to God. I was terrified that I would let Him down.

Another obstacle for me was that I felt like a complete stranger to myself. I listened to the words coming from my mouth, words describing God's enormous mercy and compassion in not giving up on me, and I wondered, *Could this really be me, Debbie Turner, who never before felt comfortable in church because I did not understand the relationship with God that seemed to fill everyone else?* Now my greatest desire had become to share Christ with others, and the church had become my refuge, a place where I felt infused with complete peace and comfort.

My old support systems were gone. I needed new ones and fast! Recognizing that I was helpless alone, I began a quest for knowledge that included attending worship services regularly. I enrolled in Bible studies. I read voraciously every Christian book I could get my hands on and began listening to Christian radio and talking to God continuously throughout the day. The closer I drew to God, the more at peace I felt. I can't say that my grief disappeared. It will never leave me. I miss Stephen terribly and I cry for him often. Occasionally, I still get blindsided by a memory or event that sends me into a tailspin, but I have learned to reach for God during those times. He calms me and helps me to deal with my loss. I am no longer consumed by my grief.

Once my faith was firmly established, I discovered another challenge. Upon accepting that heaven was indeed a real place and Stephen was there, I was ready to go! I now believed completely in God and trusted His Word. I was ready to be done with this mess of a world and began eagerly searching the sky for the second coming. "Roll back those clouds, God! I am ready to see Jesus!" I would not have been surprised at all for it to happen at any moment.

In fact, what did surprise me is that it didn't happen. I was disappointed. After a few weeks of great anticipation, I gradually began to realize that perhaps God had a longer-term plan for me. He was not going to accelerate His timing just because I had finally "gotten it" and was ready to go. The purpose He had in mind might actually require that I learn to live with what had happened and apply my new insight to help others reach the same glorious conclusions. "You mean I have to stay here?" I asked Him incredulously. I wasn't convinced that was such a good plan. There I go again, revealing to you my persistent arrogant and selfish nature. Please have patience with me. I am a work in progress and there is much still to be done within me!

Obviously, this was going to be more difficult than I had originally thought. However, I was committed to walking with the Lord, and with God's help would learn to deal with the pain. It has not been easy, but I am continuing to mature in Christ and now can honestly say that, like Paul, I am torn between the two. "For to me, to live is Christ and to die is gain." (Philippians 1:21)

What I, in my selfishness, had failed to consider, was that people all over the world are inviting Christ into their lives every day. To wish for the rapture for my own sake would mean eternal suffering for all those left behind. As much as I long to see Jesus and reach an end to my pain, I cannot wish for something that results in the removal of all hope for others. Moreover, as my wounded heart begins to heal, I am discovering that I have a meaningful role to play in God's plan of salvation, just as you do.

Considering how God reached out to me, it seems only natural to me that I would turn and accept His embrace. But I had a choice, the same choice He makes available to everyone. I could have rejected Him and chosen instead to rely on my own human logic and reasoning. A rational mind might conclude that supernatural things do not happen, and that all of my signs from God were mere coincidence.

If I had made that choice, I have no doubt that I would be dead today or making it through each day numbed by a cocktail of medications. God saved me from certain misery and failure. As I share what He has done for me, I am awestruck and amazed by the impact my story has on others. Each time someone takes a moment to tell me that my experience has touched their heart and brought them closer to God, I weep. God can use me. Now that is something worth living for!

I have come to realize that the expected human response to a tragedy is for the people involved to blame God for their misfortune. Anger is a recognized component of grieving. When we are hurt, we become desperate to understand why, and we look for someone to blame. In the absence of a human adversary, we blame God. Why did He allow this to happen to us? He could have prevented this tragedy, we reason to ourselves.

My gratitude to the Lord seems to take people by surprise.

In time, I realized that while I would never have wished for pain to touch Stephen's life or for my family to suffer his loss, God's way is the best way. Suppose God had given me a choice, one option being that Stephen would live a long life and I could see him and talk with him as much as I liked, yet for all of those years he would be tormented by drug addiction and depression. Or alternatively, God could remove Stephen from his painful circumstances by taking him to heaven where he would be enveloped in love and indescribable joy, something he could never have found here. Although the separation that I must endure would be agony, I would have the assurance that within a few years I would be reunited with him to live forever. My choice would be clear. I would not hesitate for a moment to choose immediate happiness for my child despite the cost to myself.

It saddens me when I hear of people blaming God for their

misfortune when the true perpetrator is Satan. I believe with all my heart that God reaches out to everyone in his or her darkest moments. There is no reason for Him to be there so powerfully for me and not for everyone. However, while God is reaching out to you, Satan is simultaneously using every possible diversion to thwart your acceptance. There is a battle raging every moment. Scripture tells us in Ephesians 6:12, "For our struggle is not against flesh and blood, but against the rulers, against the authorities, against the powers of this dark world and against the spiritual forces of evil in the heavenly realms."

Do I feel anger? Oh yes, I feel a powerful, purpose-defining anger. My child did not begin his life fighting drug addiction and depression. Stephen was a delightful and gifted young man and I place the responsibility for what happened to him precisely where it belongs: on Satan. He is solely to blame for stealing the beautiful light from Stephen's eyes. I won't forget that for a moment.

Nor will I forget the One who saved him. The gratitude and love I feel for my Lord, the One who rescued my child, is immeasurable. Satan may have thought he was enjoying a red-letter moment on the night Stephen committed suicide, but his evil glee was fleeting. God claimed the true victory. He welcomed Stephen into heaven and at the same time gained a dedicated believer in me, one who will never be silenced.

So how does this desire to serve God, combined with a sense of awkwardness, translate into effective discipleship? One step at a time.

So do not fear, for I am with you;
do not be dismayed, for I am your God.
I will strengthen you and help you;
I will uphold you with my righteous right hand.
All who rage against you
will surely be ashamed and disgraced;
those who oppose you
will be as nothing and perish.
Though you search for your enemies,
you will not find them.
Those who wage war against you
will be as nothing at all.
For I am the Lord, your God,
who takes hold of your right hand
and says to you, Do not fear;
I will help you.
Isaiah 41:10-13

Chapter 8

Learning to Walk

Have you ever had the pleasure of observing a young child as he takes his very first steps? Wide eyes bright with excitement and fear, he releases his clenched fingers and with trembling legs catapults across the room. The distance traveled on this maiden journey isn't important, only the fact that he is mobile! There's so much to see, so many places to explore. Fall down? No problem. He is not giving up. With fierce determination he pushes himself back to his feet and tries it again. He has little control or sense of direction at first, but that comes quickly. His discovery is powered by a tremendous desire, a hunger to do what he has seen all the big people around him do—walk!

The first steps described here parallel those of a new Christian. Hesitant at first, we step forth on wobbly legs to explore this new person we have become. Fired by a thirst for Jesus we plunge forward, not completely sure what we are supposed to do or even how to do it, but fueled by a tremendous desire. Yes, there is fear and uncertainty, but we are driven by a hunger to know God and to discover His will in our lives.

Unhindered, both the toddler and the new Christian will learn to walk with sure, firm footsteps. Weak legs and confidence gradually grow stronger. Soon we can travel anywhere we wish! Not content with mere walking, we learn to run, to leap, and to dance. Parents watch with delight as their child grows in strength and experience, just as the new believer develops in faith and understanding under the loving care of a heavenly Father.

For most babies, learning to walk occurs naturally as in the scene described above. But suppose for a moment that there is a malevolent force hiding in the room, one whose sole mission is to make absolutely certain that this child does not learn to walk, ever. Imagine that each time the child's trembling legs take a step, he is violently knocked to the floor. Happiness turns to hurt. Stunned eyes fill with tears as loud wails fill the room. As the cycle continues the wails diminish to whining, to whimpers, and eventually to the terrible, deafening silence of utter discouragement. The child gives up. He is defeated. The wistful longing is never completely extinguished but has been pushed deep inside where it can be ignored.

"Perhaps," he tells himself, "I am not meant to walk or run or dance. I will learn to be content with sitting. Sitting is comfortable. And it is safe. No one knocks me down or tries to hurt me here."

What a waste of potential. And how accurately it describes Satan's agenda towards believers. Having failed in his attempts to separate you from God, he becomes more determined than ever to prevent you from leading any others to Christ. If you become a fully functioning and effective witness, what havoc you could wreak on his plans. He is all too familiar with the power that would be unleashed within you and he fears it! You must be stopped.

What is his plan? To attack while you are vulnerable, still finding your way and feeling a little out of place. You haven't yet learned to recognize your Father's voice or to tap into His strength.

What is Satan's weapon of choice? The voice inside your head that maliciously whispers that you were not meant to walk or run: *You are unworthy. You cannot do what you think God told you to do. You lack ability. You lack resources, opportunity, and strength. And most of all, you lack guidance from God. How do you know what God wants you to do? What if you are wrong? What if you try and fail? How humiliating. People will laugh at you. You will probably just become an obstacle and hindrance to God. You are lucky just to be saved. Better hope He doesn't notice you at all and regret calling you His own. Just sit there quietly. Anything more is too risky.*

Satan doesn't stop at tormenting you with your own self-defeating thoughts. He isn't picky. He'll use others: your spouse; your relatives; your teachers; your friends. One of these is bound to do the trick. Imagine the voice of someone you love and respect belittling your faith and chipping away at your confidence. If he can find any opening at all, you won't have to imagine it. That voice will ring in your ears long after the words have actually been spoken. And by the way, Satan is an equal opportunity employer. He may even use well-intentioned but misguided believers to block your path. He is ruthless and persistent. If you are on fire for God, then make no mistake about it, Satan is fired up about you. You are a target.

Let's suppose that the doubts combined with a lack of support from others were insufficient to knock you down. Well done, but don't become overconfident. He has been known to mix in a pinch of illness, a dash of financial problems, or even a cup of conflict, and perhaps all at once. This enemy has studied your weaknesses.

How do you fight back? It's simple: you don't. You are not strong enough to win the battle, but God is. His hand is always extended to you to pull you from the fray if you will just grab hold. Why don't we see it? Simply because most of the time we are not even looking! His hand is hidden behind our clouds of self-sufficiency. In our society we are taught to make it on our own. So we stand on trembling legs, begin to walk, and when we get knocked down enough times we learn to stay there.

It was tempting for me to stay down. My heart and spirit were mortally wounded and I could not bear more stress or problems. I certainly wasn't up to overcoming any challenges. Satan called to me, tempting me to just let go: *sink into depression ... stay in bed and cry. Use tranquilizers and alcohol to numb the pain. No one will blame you. Perhaps you should even consider suicide yourself.*

I considered every one of those things, more than once. I was lured by the call and the promise of an end to the pain. I wallowed in that pit of despondency for a while, but then I pulled myself out of it.

How was I able to do this? Where did I find the strength and courage to keep walking? Did I reach deep into my inner resources and determine that my life was worth living? No. There was little chance of that occurring.

No, God took me by the hand and lifted me up. Then He led me forward one small step at a time.

Remember the childhood story of Hansel and Gretel, the children who were delivered from the perils of the forest by faithfully following a meandering trail of breadcrumbs? My world has become like theirs, a meandering trail of breadcrumbs that God has carefully placed before me to lead me past the danger into the safety of His arms. I move to one and then to another, stopping momentarily to get my bearings and to spot the next one just ahead. He doesn't require that I stumble around blindly in the dark. The trail only seems meandering to me because from my perspective, I cannot see God's entire plan or even a complete view of my place within it. And that is fine with me. This is where God calls upon us to trust Him. "Do you trust me?" He says. "Have I not proven my love and compassion for you?" Slowly I began to relinquish my need to be in control, and I learned to submit to His guidance. I am not required to understand, just to believe, to trust, and to obey when He speaks to me.

I promised you details and I intend to deliver. "How does He speak to you?" you ask. "Is His voice audible?" I wish He did speak to me audibly! That would go a long way towards silencing those fiendish doubts Satan uses in an attempt to discourage me. I could adapt quite nicely to hearing heavenly instructions whispered in my ear. But no, most often He speaks to me now in the form of persistent, even somewhat nagging thoughts that refuse to be ignored. I actually think they have been tests of a sort, designed to measure and then to strengthen my faith.

I have already shared with you how God spoke to me through dreams and by moving inanimate objects. The first time I heard Him as one of these thoughts, the situation involved someone associated with my company whom I learned had become the victim of a theft. Her purse was robbed of six hundred dollars, and for her a loss of that amount was staggering.

Almost immediately upon learning of her situation, I thought to myself, "You need to give her some money to help her with this." The amount I felt led to give her was very specific. At first, I am ashamed to say, I was resistant. It wasn't even the entire amount that had been stolen. I told myself that I didn't even know her. I needed that money for other things, and besides that, she probably had family that would help her.

Still, I could not get her out of my mind. A weekend passed and I became increasingly consumed with guilt. I began comparing my personal financial situation with hers to the point that it was driving me crazy! Finally, I drove to the bank and withdrew the money. I called her and asked her to come to my office. She arrived within minutes. I began the conversation by asking her how she was coping financially. She told me about her struggles to raise her children and a nephew, and how losing that much money was a devastating blow to her. I sympathized with her. Yet when I asked if she had any idea who had stolen the money, she expressed no bitterness. She blamed herself for carrying that much money in her purse and for failing to be more cautious.

I explained that the reason I had asked her to meet me was that God had laid upon my heart a desire to help her. I handed her the money and she was speechless. At first she tried to give it back to me. When she realized I was serious, she counted it and began to cry. She said, "This is the amount of my rent that is due!" I will never as long as I live forget that moment. The first sacrifice God asked of me was returned to me in blessings a hundredfold. He flooded me with such feelings of warmth and approval that my eyes fill with tears just thinking of it.

Don't think for a moment that my behavior in this situation was admirable or remarkable. I did not approach the Lord's directive with an eager and willing spirit. In fact, my actions were motivated more by my desire to silence the persistent voice in my head than for any altruistic reasons. Despite my reluctance, I did obey, and He rewarded my obedience with the assurance of His approval. I learned an important lesson from this experience and vowed to be quicker to respond the next time He asked me to do something.

It wasn't long before He gave me another opportunity.

"Lord, if it's you," Peter replied,
"tell me to come to you on the water."
"Come," he said.
Then Peter got down out of the boat,
walked on the water and came toward Jesus.
But when he saw the wind, he was afraid and,
beginning to sink, cried out,
"Lord, save me!"
Immediately Jesus reached out his hand
and caught him.
"You of little faith," he said,
"why did you doubt?"
Matthew 14:28-31

Chapter 9

Stepping Out of the Boat

By the time I reached the age of forty-two, years of self reflection had revealed to me at least a partial understanding of my own weaknesses. Regrettably, my past performance in withstanding temptation or even in maintaining convictions had been less than stellar. I recognized within myself a tendency to develop a sudden passion to do something or to acquire a particular item, and that desire would consume me until I possessed it. Predictably, then I would lose interest once the possession was mine. While capable of intense focus, I often lacked staying power.

One aspect of Christianity that had previously frightened me away from God was the commitment required, the realization that it would be all or nothing. To admit the existence of God and then to deliberately ignore Him was inconceivable, so I avoided the question. When I did consider the possibility, I left it at that, just a possibility. A "Possible God" did not require anything of me.

With the sudden and unexpected death of my son, I was forced to deal with the question, "Once and for all, is there a God?" It loomed before me, and God tenderly placed the answer directly before me where I could not miss it unless I deliberately chose to do so. To fail this test would have required that I intentionally blind myself to His presence. Unfortunately, some do. I had done so many times in the past. In fact, blinding myself to God had become an established pattern for me.

Have you ever experienced a powerful tugging upon your heart spawned by the truth of a pastor's words, or from the very sight of some natural wonder? Have you found yourself unexpectedly fighting tears as your soul is stirred by the beauty of a song? I have and then deliberately turned away. I can vividly recall the first time I heard the Christian band Mercy Me sing "I Can Only Imagine." I was driving and had just turned my car onto the road that runs behind my office when that song began to play on the radio. Listening to the words, I felt so overcome with emotion that I considered pulling to the curb and parking the car so I could deal with the conviction I was feeling. For a moment, I felt a tremendous desire to confront my feelings about God and determine why a song dealing with heaven would bring tears to my eyes. But I didn't do it. I swallowed hard and drove on. Suppose I had given in to that impulse instead of hardening my heart? Would anything have been different? There were other missed opportunities and numerous occasions when God stood knocking at my door, calling me to return to Him. But I refused to listen. "Not today, God. I have too many important things to do."

That all changed the day my fast-paced world came to a screeching halt. And where was God now? Knocking again. Praise God, He didn't give up on me! This time, I threw the door open wide and fell into His arms. The moment I opened my heart to Him, He flooded my spirit with mercy and drenched me in a tidal wave of grace. His love lifted me up and sent me spinning like a leaf caught in the path of a bursting dam.

It seems implausible yet I actually felt His delight in my return to Him. I was the prodigal child who had set out to do life my way and I had failed. Now I had returned to my Father and the incredible assurance that despite my rebellion, He had never stopped loving me. I was overwhelmed.

Gratitude filled my heart and I vowed to demonstrate my appreciation to Him, but knowing my history, I feared that my old tendencies would resurface. I did not want to let Him down. I desperately feared that I would fail Him by forgetting the magnitude of what He had done for me, or that I would settle so comfortably into the safety of my pew that I would not reveal Him to others. God had quite literally saved my life and not only mine. My life was of the least importance to me. He had saved my son for all eternity. There was nothing more critical to me! If I failed to serve Him with every ounce of my strength, I would be unable to bear the shame.

So where was I to begin? I didn't know anything about this world that was governed by an all-knowing, all-seeing, all-loving God. As days and then weeks passed, I began to see increasing evidence of God revealed in my daily life. I sensed that I was moving towards something and could not dispel the feeling that God was preparing me in a steady, deliberate way to fulfill a specific purpose for Him. *How am I to discover His plan?* I wondered.

First I had to accept that it was not my job to discover His plan but to simply be receptive to His guidance. Making the transition from leader to trusting follower was contrary to my nature so, admittedly, that step was a struggle. My career required organization, and I was accustomed to setting goals and working from a clearly defined plan. Second, I wanted to learn as much as possible about Him by studying His Word, and I wanted it now! I had a lot of catching up to do. Third, I realized the importance of developing a strong support system to encourage me and to help me if I began to veer off track.

Again, God abundantly provided everything I needed. Multiple opportunities for learning were available to me: Christian radio and CDs, thought-provoking books and Bible studies, supportive family and friends, and most important of all, a Holy Spirit-filled church. Although these faith-strengthening aids were easily accessible to me, with the exception of my family who has consistently been there by my side, I had to consciously seek them out.

Developing a relationship with God requires intent and effort. But, oh the rewards! By the middle of February I felt that I was ready to begin attending church. The pastor of my sister's church had performed Stephen's funeral service, and I felt a special connection to him because of the insight and sensitivity he had demonstrated concerning our loss. My husband and I visited his church and were immediately welcomed by the congregation.

My love and devotion for my Lord grew steadily as I learned more about Him. I joined a women's Bible study of *The Purpose Driven Life* just as they were concluding the last three sessions. It was a small group, less than a dozen. I had already read the book by this time since a Christian friend had given me a copy following Stephen's death, and was looking forward with great anticipation to learning from the other ladies who were participants in the study. My intent was to sit quietly and to benefit from their experience. However, I failed to consult God about His plan. At the end of the first session, the ladies asked for volunteers to lead a chapter at the next meeting. Seeing that they had fewer volunteers than remaining chapters, I agreed to accept one.

Upon arriving home, I settled onto the sofa to read my assigned chapter and to discover precisely what I had gotten myself into. The topic of my chapter was sharing your testimony with others. Again, I sensed the Holy Spirit leading me to complete a specific task. Try as I might, I could not silence the thought that God wanted me to use this opportunity to share what He had done in my life. And, oh how I tried to silence it! Or more accurately, Satan tried to silence me. Doubts and insecurities assailed me: *These ladies do not know you, have no interest in your life and will think you are trying to take over. You always have to control things, don't you, Debbie? It is always about you. You haven't seen anyone else do this. Just lead the chapter like they are expecting you to do.*

I was terrified and fretted over it the entire week but the thought was too insistent to ignore. When the time came for me to present the chapter, I did so following the established pattern. Then I took a deep breath and forged ahead. I told the group that I had something I needed to share with them. I explained that I had recently lost my son to suicide. I spoke slowly and resolutely, barely daring to look at them. I described my anguish, the feelings of hopelessness and desperation that threatened to consume me, and finally the many wondrous ways in which God had revealed Himself to me and comforted me. By the time I finished I was in tears and struggling to speak. I hesitantly raised my eyes and was amazed to see that their faces were also wet with tears. Additionally, I saw revealed within their eyes complete understanding, sympathy, and acceptance. Their response was immediate and tremendously reassuring to me. They thanked me for revealing my personal struggle to them and spoke of how my story inspired them and drew them closer to the Lord.

I had shared these experiences with the Lord with my family and with my employees, but this was the first time I had revealed so much to complete strangers and witnessed the impact it could have on others. From that moment on they were strangers no longer. Each one became a loving and supportive friend.

Afterwards, as I drove the short distance to my house, I marveled at the feelings of wonder and joy that were flooding my heart. Miraculously, God had used me to encourage others, and He rewarded my obedience by opening my eyes to the possibility of a purpose for the rest of my life. Me, of all people! Could I really be used to make a tangible difference for God in the lives of others? Somehow, despite the horror of my circumstances, I realized that burning within me was a sense of fulfillment that was vastly different from anything I had experienced before. Never had there been a feeling to compare with this. And it came not from any personal achievement or recognition but instead from my willingness to shine a spotlight on what God had done despite my failure.

Within weeks I was confronted with an even more daunting challenge. I returned home from a subsequent Bible study to learn from my husband that a young lady we knew casually had attempted suicide earlier in the day. She was hospitalized and, as of late evening, the doctors had been unable to awaken her.

I entered our bedroom and fell to my knees in prayer for her. This simply could not happen! She was still alive, and where there is life, there is hope for change. I promised God that if she survived I would talk to her about what He had done for me. I would reveal to her that there is a loving God who can help her with her problems, and that there is a far better way out of her agony than the one she had chosen.

I won't attempt to minimize my fear. The idea of becoming involved in an attempted suicide shook me to the core. I wasn't confident at all of my ability to handle my intense emotions surrounding the situation, yet I fell asleep that night knowing that I must speak to her.

The following morning I placed a call to her fiancé. He told me that she was now awake but in intensive care and was expected to be in the hospital for several weeks for counseling. I asked him to keep me informed and promised that once she was allowed to have visitors outside of the family, I would visit her.

He immediately responded that she could have visitors that very day. In fact, he wanted me to see her right away. I hesitated. So soon? I had not expected this. I felt a trembling begin deep within me. Could I do this? I knew I had to help, so I agreed to visit her that afternoon.

Throughout the day I prayed continuously, especially during the drive to the hospital. "Father, please provide me with the right words to say to her. I have never done anything like this before, and the consequences of a mistake are so grave." I could sense Him reassuring me and strengthening my resolve. I could count on Him to be with me every step of the way, and through Him I knew I could do this. On the drive over I stopped briefly at the "Shepherd's Shoppe," a Christian bookstore, and purchased a small New Testament Bible for her. I repeated my pleas for strength as I pulled into the parking lot of the hospital. Rounding the curve, I spied a vacant spot in the front row of parking spaces. How fortunate and extremely rare in this lot, I thought. It was the only vacant spot in sight. I pulled to a stop and switched off the ignition. Then I noticed the car parked on my right.

There it sat, shining bright red in the sunlight. A Ford Taurus, the same model and color as Stephen's car. I sat very still looking at it and then smiled as my eyes filled with tears. Once again, God had visibly made His presence known to me just when I most needed His reassurance.

Was this a mere coincidence again? After all, the Taurus was one of the most popular cars on the road at the time. It's possible I suppose, but how likely could it be that I was suddenly swimming in a sea of random coincidences? Events like these had never occurred to me before. And statistical probability couldn't explain the certainty blooming in my heart. Surely by now you also recognize the weakness in these arguments of coincidence. At some point it becomes more difficult to deny the evidence of God than it does to believe. That critical point had long since come and gone for me!

As promised, God carried me. I remember little of the walk to the intensive care unit, but I do remember whispering a final prayer as the elevator carried me to her floor. Her family left the room soon after I arrived and suddenly, I was alone with her. I pulled a chair to the side of her bed and held her hand. She turned to me and I caught my breath at the pain swimming in her eyes. The despair evident there tore at my heart, reminding me of another's. I began to talk, hesitantly at first but with increasing confidence as I shared my strong faith in God and my conviction that He could help her. She listened without a word as I stressed that He had a purpose for her that far surpassed the life she had experienced thus far. Before departing, I prayed with her, asking God to protect her and draw her near to Him. I was encouraged when she told me that she did believe in God.

After talking with her for a short while, I left her. As I drove away I again experienced the warm blanket of God's approval. Not that I had done everything right. My words did not resonate with wisdom and experience, only with heartfelt conviction. There were questions I failed to ask and truths I forgot to reveal. However, I was obedient despite my fear and that is all God required of me. That is also all He asks of you. Confidence will grow with experience, and He will put the words into our mouths that He wishes for us to share. Remember, it is the Holy Spirit who convicts a heart, not us. Our responsibility is to plant the seeds of faith and reveal Christ through our words and behavior.

God had tested me. Would I follow even when it was frightening and uncomfortable for me? So far I was doing okay. I began to hunger for more.

Then I heard the voice of the Lord saying,
"Whom shall I send?
And who will go for us?"
And I said, "Here am I. Send me!"
Isaiah 6:8

When the angel of the Lord appeared to Gideon,
he said, "The Lord is with you, mighty warrior."
"But Lord," Gideon asked, "how can I save Israel?
My clan is the weakest in Manasseh,
and I am the least in my family."
Judges 6:12,15

Chapter 10

No Turning Back

A s I consider my emotions during this time, I am struck by their paradoxical intensity. On the one hand, I felt like the child I was back in elementary school, frantically waving my hand to get the teacher's attention as if to say, *Pick me! Pick me! Let me lead the lunch line; let me pass out the papers!*

By June, I recognized an identical and persistent longing, but this time as an adult Christian: *Use me, God! Allow me to give something back to your kingdom in appreciation for what you are doing for me. Show me that I have a purpose, and that there is still a reason for me to be.*

On the other hand, I felt insecure and unworthy. For goodness sakes, as we say in the South, I was still struggling to sort out the order of the books in the Bible! On Sunday mornings when the pastor instructed us to turn to a particular scripture, I would turn towards the back when I should have turned towards the front. How could I have any degree of credibility in helping others come to know Christ? I was hopelessly unprepared and there was so much to learn!

Consider my dilemma. As much as I feared that God might not want to use me, I also feared that He would! The fact that I was caught in such a quandary at all was indicative of the radical reorientation I had experienced in my life.

Have you also struggled with inner conflict? Have you ever reached a point in time when you recognized that you had moved beyond your old, safe, comfort zone and were now plunging headfirst towards the unknown? The fear can be paralyzing.

Think of the proverbial kitten stuck in a tree. A persistent longing beckoned, drawing you forward, so you stepped out onto the branch and went further than you had ever before explored. How exciting! Until the moment you looked down and then quickly back towards the safety of the tree realizing how far you had traveled. Inevitably the fear assails you with panicky thoughts: *I am actually hanging out on a limb here! This is risky! Should I go backwards? Forward?* Indecision prevails so you stay put, shivering and waiting for rescue.

My heart's desire was to serve God, but how? I had spent the decades skirting what I thought of as the "Christian World." That life had always been close by, within my sight, yet I didn't have the desire to become a part of it or even know how to do so if I did want to join in. I struggled with indecision. *Does God want me to turn my back on the secular world altogether? Should I abandon my livelihood, my lucrative business? Should I enter fulltime missions or the ministry?*

As I mentioned previously, my natural tendency is to commit myself either completely or not at all to everything I do.

I prayed, asking for guidance and discernment to make the right decisions. God responded by providing more opportunities for me to witness to others in my current role. As each experience with God unfolded in my life, I immediately shared the details with my family and coworkers. I felt encouraged to witness the impact that my growing relationship with God could have on someone else. Friends began dropping by the office to offer comfort and support during my loss. I eagerly met every opportunity by also sharing with them how I had come to know the Lord, and how His power was providing me with the strength to go on. Amazingly enough, by the end of each visit, my friends left telling me that I had ministered to them as much if not more so than they had to me!

After testing my willingness to share with individuals and with the small group in our Bible study, God decided this message was destined for a broader audience. Forget safety and my comfort zone! God had different plans. Would I remain obedient to Him if the stakes were higher and if following Him in obedience involved risk?

God next chose to test my resolve in a business setting. The Rotary Club to which I belong traditionally begins each meeting with an invocation. I had been asked to lead the invocation at a meeting two years ago but considering my lack of a relationship with God at the time, I had immediately declined using the excuse that I would feel too uncomfortable praying in public. I failed to mention that obviously I felt uncomfortable praying in private as well since I rarely did so.

The last week of June 2004, I was sitting with a group of fellow members at a club meeting, relaxing and enjoying the fellowship, when the designated member approached the podium to begin the invocation.

Suddenly, as though it was whispered into my ear, was the thought, *You need to do that.*

I imagine the expression on my face must have been one of sheer horror! If anyone had been watching during the following internal exchange, they would certainly have called for a doctor!

I feigned ignorance stalling for time, *Do what?*

Very simply, "That."

You have got to be kidding! You are asking me to hijack the invocation and to use the opportunity to tell this group of 120 business professionals what You have done in my life? Many of them are my clients!

Again calmly, "Yes, you need to do that."

99

Lord, please, they will think I am crazy! I think I am crazy! That is not what we do during the invocation. We simply recite a nice, non-threatening, respectable prayer asking You to bless the food, and then we open the meeting! Nothing emotional. This is not the right setting for that!

"Everywhere is the right setting. You need to do that."

I sat battling silently with myself for the remainder of the meeting, completely oblivious to the speaker and to the others sitting around me.

I did not audibly hear God's voice. However, as mentioned previously, I have learned through personal experience and have had it confirmed repeatedly that God can and does voice His guidance through persistent thoughts that will not be ignored.

This was one I desperately wanted to ignore!

At first I opted for partial obedience. As I drove back to my office, I conceded that as soon as I reached my desk I would compose a prayer if He would provide the words, and the two of us would just think about this awhile longer. Frankly, I was hoping He would recognize the difficulty of such a task and abandon the idea altogether.

Once seated, I reluctantly placed my fingers on the keyboard certain that I would think of nothing to write. God knew better. Like a mighty wave, words poured into my consciousness and I typed frantically, trying to record them as quickly as possible. In a short time the prayer was finished. I sat very still, staring at the words glowing innocently on my computer monitor. I shook my head slowly from side to side. "God" I said, "this is just not done."

Over the next two weeks, I sought advice from my mother and my sister. Both came down firmly on the side of God. There was no escaping it. Once written, the words of this prayer haunted my every waking thought. While working, eating, reading, and sleeping I thought of this prayer.

Another possible out occurred to me. As a test, I would contact the committee chair who was responsible for scheduling the invocation and ask him if there were any openings on the calendar for me to volunteer for the role. I decided that if God really wanted me to do this, He would open a door. If not, and if the schedule was already filled, I would be absolved from this responsibility. Holding my breath in fearful anticipation, I dialed the number. Suffice it to say that God has a sense of humor! The committee chair was thrilled to hear from me. He assured me that the very next meeting at the end of July was available. In fact, not only was the next meeting available, but since our fiscal year had just begun, he had the entire year to fill!

I could not prevent a smile. "Okay God," I agreed, "You have made it abundantly clear that You want me to do this, so let's proceed together." Once His will was confirmed, I accepted my fate and discovered that my apprehension and reluctance completely vanished. Three weeks remained in which to prepare. Since I was committed to doing this, it must be done right. God had chosen to announce His presence at a Rotary meeting through me of all people. Admittedly this event didn't carry the significance of, say, Moses and the burning bush, but still, I did not want to mess it up! The prayer itself was complete. However, I had no idea what I would say before just plunging into it.

God had brought me safely to this point, so I decided to leave it in His hands and trust that He would reveal His message to me in plenty of time. A week passed. It was now two weeks before the date and still I had no idea of what to say before the prayer.

I prayed, "God, remember me? You know, I'm the one You got into this mess. I have to do this thing in two weeks. I am obeying You, but I could use a little help here!"

Then when I least expected it, He delivered the text directly into my mind. Complete. Precisely the way I would speak it two weeks later. As unlikely a place as it may be for a spiritual revelation, God selected the solitude of a tanning bed to speak to me. I had just adjusted the radio to a Christian station and closed my eyes when the words began to circulate lazily through my thoughts, completely blocking the sound of the radio. There were no doubts or hesitation, just a deliberate unfolding of an idea as though I were reading it from a script. I repeated the paragraphs to myself three or four times, and as soon as the timer rang I got up and hurriedly recorded them on the back of a crumpled bank envelope I found in my purse. The entire presentation was instantly memorized.

Everything fit together and it felt right. Another week passed.

Seven days to go and the fear came flooding back. There I was, hanging out on a limb, just like the kitten. It was time for a decision to be made.

The next step was critical and I knew it. Safety lay behind me, or at least the illusion of safety. I could step forward into the unknown, comforted by the assurance that I had the full backing of God; nevertheless, it would be a step into uncharted waters.

Or I could still turn back. After all, I was comfortable in my current position. Why should I rock the boat? The people who would be in attendance at this meeting are my professional peers, and many of them are clients of my firm. Most are men. I couldn't be certain of their reaction to such a personal account, especially one possessing such a religious theme. This invocation would be a definitive departure from their expectations. Was that wise? Was it a sensible thing to do? I could find a nice safe invocation to read and no one would know the difference.

It was my choice completely. God never forces us to obey. It was entirely up to me.

I weighed the arguments but ultimately concluded that God had given me instructions and, sensible or not, I was going to follow them. I was called to deliver the message God had provided to me. That is all. Just stand where I was supposed to stand and move my mouth. He did not need or want me to do anything more. God was responsible for managing how this message would be received in the hearts of those in attendance, not I.

Finally the moment arrived, and I approached the podium clutching my Bible like the life preserver it actually is. In my career, I have been forced to overcome the fear of speaking in public or at least appear that I have. However, this was very different. In just a few seconds I would share an intensely personal experience with a group of people who had no idea they were about to hear it. My hands were shaking badly. I sent a quick prayer heavenward asking for a steady voice and for Him to provide me with the strength to avoid tears.

I began to speak and the room grew eerily silent. No one moved. I could hear no shuffling feet or clinking silverware. I recited the introduction from memory and then read the prayer. Each time I rehearsed, I had desperately struggled to fight tears when I said, "From the day Stephen was born, he held my heart in his hands." In this setting I feared that dissolving in tears would undermine my message, so I was trying very hard to maintain my composure. Somehow I made it through with only a brief crack in my voice at that critical part.

The complete text of that message is inserted here:

"I would like to begin by sharing with you an incident that occurred a couple of years ago. I was walking into one of our meetings when someone approached me and asked if I would consider leading the invocation at a future meeting."

"I can still recall my reaction vividly: I thought to myself, "Who me? Uh-uh."

"What I said aloud was, "'I am sorry, but I would feel too uncomfortable praying in public.'"

"I am here today to tell you that a lot can change in a couple of years. In fact, a life can be changed in a single moment."

"This time I asked for the opportunity to lead the invocation. I did so because I want to say 'Thank You' in the most meaningful way possible to so many of you who have provided support to me during the loss of my son … and also because I want to point clearly to the source of my strength."

"I have heard it said that once you have a child, from that point forward, it feels as though your heart has grown arms and legs and is running loose outside of your body. I have always thought that was a perfect description of my love for my children."

"I can tell you that there is only one reason I am able to survive Stephen's loss, and not only survive, but to find happiness and meaning in life."

"It is because I know this story does not end here. You see, I have skipped ahead and read the back of the Book. **The ending is awesome!**"

"Please pray with me:
Our heavenly Father,
Thank You for bringing the people of this club into my life and for blessing me with such compassionate and supportive friends.

I have witnessed them give selflessly of their time and resources to people in need, most of whom are complete strangers to them. Then, when tragedy struck one of their own, they were right here beside me offering comfort and asking what they could do to help.

I thank you sincerely for surrounding me with people who are always available with a warm hug, a ready smile, a sympathetic ear and the wisdom to verbally acknowledge my pain. Only You truly understand how much that has meant to me.

I ask that You take this spirit of compassion that You have placed in their hearts and continue to multiply it throughout our community and even our world.

Above all, Lord, I thank You for revealing Yourself to me in mighty ways following the loss of my son.

Father, You know that from the day Stephen was born, he held my heart in his hands.

You reached deep into the nightmare of his death and bestowed upon me the most incredible gift I could hope for—the certainty that one day I will be reunited with him and will never have to fear losing him again.

Thank you for giving me strength and courage when my own were woefully inadequate and for using this devastating loss to change me in ways I would never have dreamed possible. Allow me to be a living testament to Your power and leave no doubt that, without You, I would not be standing here today.

I pray for all of us when I ask that You strengthen our faith so that when trouble comes, we learn to seek the gift that lies within the challenge and discover the valuable lessons it holds for our character.

Lord, I ask that You continue to reveal Your presence to me and to everyone here today. Let us reflect Your love in all we do. We humbly ask that You use our lives and our activities through Rotary to Your glory.

In Jesus' name I pray, Amen"

I tucked my notes into my Bible and lifted my eyes to measure their reaction.

Undoubtedly, God's presence filled this room. Many were fighting tears or brushing them from their eyes, men and women alike.

As I returned to my seat, a gentleman reached across from another table and shook my hand. Several others mouthed the words "Thank you" as they met my gaze, and a friend stopped by my table to give me a hug as she left the stage. As soon as the meeting concluded, I was encircled by friends who were anxious to offer their comfort and to share their appreciation for my courage. If they only knew!

I had no courage. I simply trusted God even when it didn't make sense to do so, and He was proven right. The message I had so feared to share was welcomed and was also what our group most needed to hear. Imagine that! Were all present moved by my situation? I doubt it. But enough were that even now, several months later, I continue to be approached by members who thank me for being so openly vulnerable and bold about pointing to the source of my strength.

This was a significant turning point for me. Stepping out in faith meant subjecting my behavior to intense scrutiny from that day forward. I had chosen to publicly align myself with God and to speak of the difference He was making in my life. Those could not be empty words. I must demonstrate a difference in my life, daily. There must be a consistent and visible change.

One change I made was to eliminate alcohol from my life. Almost without an intentional decision to do so, I stopped drinking completely. Since I did not consume alcohol frequently, this was not a drastic change for me. I enjoyed an occasional cocktail or glass of wine with dinner or at a social function. Now, realizing the role that alcohol and drugs played in the loss of my son as well as my dear brother eleven years previously, I developed an intense distaste for it. I felt repelled by the thought, and furthermore did not want to compromise my witness to others if I was seen engaging in a questionable activity.

One evening my husband and I were having dinner at a local restaurant when our discussion turned towards the subject of drinking alcohol. He didn't understand why having a glass of wine with our meal was a problem for me. I had just explained to him how that seemingly innocent act could have lasting consequences in compromising my witness, when we were unexpectedly provided with a living demonstration.

At that very moment, a couple whom we knew from church entered the dining room from the bar area. They were dining with another couple and three of the four were carrying mixed drinks. While not making a spectacle of themselves, they were obviously under the influence. Jasper and I observed them in silence for a moment. Then I asked, "How does seeing them drink alcohol make you feel?" Somberly, he replied, "Very disappointed."

I began to look at everything in my life differently. Whereas before I had accepted whatever our culture deemed normal as also acceptable to me, now I viewed the world through a different lens. Things I had previously enjoyed, such as certain fashion magazines, books, movies and television shows, were no longer appealing to me. I felt convicted by the Holy Spirit to make changes.

Until an event occurs in our lives that heightens our sensitivity to it, we don't realize how immersed our society has become in activities that promote the pursuit of an unhealthy and ungodly lifestyle. Observe the culture around you for a moment and note how frequently you hear references to death, suicide, unhealthy sexual relationships, and fixations on material possessions, drugs and alcohol. These messages are pervasive. Often they are disguised with humor so they appear innocuous.

It should disturb us mightily that our children are forming opinions about ethical positions and standards of conduct in part by the values our culture presents to them as normal and acceptable. Why do we allow it? Because everyone else does it?

There is something about reflecting on the glory of God that turns the spotlight of reproach inward. Rather than comparing ourselves to other people, where we may be able to reassure ourselves that we are actually "pretty good," we should compare ourselves to Christ. He is our behavior model. Don't place your faith in another human being. You most assuredly will be disappointed. I had always considered myself to be a good person. Now, when viewed from God's perspective, I was alarmed by the wicked and hateful thoughts that invaded my mind.

I began to consciously censure these thoughts, which meant I spent a lot of time asking God for forgiveness! Purposefully, I took control of each one that seemed contrary to my true feelings and rejected them. I asked God to strengthen me in my war with my own sinful nature.

Change has not always been easy, but I remain committed to God, depending on His grace to transform me day by day.

The watchman opens the gate for him,
and the sheep listen to his voice.
He calls his own sheep by name and leads them out.
When he has brought out all his own,
he goes on ahead of them, and his sheep
follow him because they know his voice.
John 10:3-4

Chapter 11

Recognizing His Voice

What does God sound like or feel like? I have experienced Him under many conditions and continue to witness new manifestations of His Presence on a regular basis. He never ceases to surprise me or to amaze me. Although the full reality of God far surpasses my limited powers of description, I will attempt as best as I can to put into words the means by which He has communicated with me.

He rescues me: My first encounters with Him after Stephen's death, although I did not recognize them immediately for what they were, filled me with love, gratitude, and peace. I felt comforted by a tidal wave of grace that sent warmth radiating through my body. The manifestations of His presence through dreams along with unexpected and unexplainable events dissolved my despair and replaced it with the assurance that everything was going to be alright.

He leads me: I have experienced His firm guiding hand in my daily activities. I have heard His inaudible voice within my heart, which calls me to action and refuses to be silenced. His voice is never demanding or domineering but quietly resolute and tinged with understanding at my reluctance.

He encourages me: I have experienced the incomparable pleasure of His approval when I have acted according to His instruction. I can only describe it as a supreme feeling of complete satisfaction, not in myself or in my own abilities but rather in a realization that I have been part of some far greater purpose.

He chastises me: Conversely, I have also felt His disapproval and conviction when I behave in a way that is contrary to His purpose. To give you an example, a couple of months ago, long after I should have known better, I did something that even now causes me shame at the thought of sharing it with you. While on my way to a business luncheon, I found myself wondering if I should just say the blessing in my car before I joined the others since I was unfamiliar with their spiritual convictions.

As soon as the thought crossed my mind, I felt horrified. I had literally pleaded with God on my knees for Him to use me for His service, and then I hesitated at saying the blessing at a lunch meeting! I immediately looked heavenward and said aloud, "I have no idea why You even put up with me. You must be constantly frustrated!" To compensate for my ignorance, I suggested to Him that I stand up and say the blessing aloud so that everyone in the restaurant could hear me. That would teach me to hide my faith! Realizing such a display would only result in attention being directed towards me rather than towards Him, I simply asked for forgiveness and asked His blessing upon my food at the table before I ate it.

He shelters me: God has been my refuge during periods of turmoil and fear. When I have felt my composure slipping away in the face of grief, I have been comforted by His strength and calming power. His "voice" reassured me that I was not alone and that there was nothing to fear.

He transforms me with His glory: I have been swept to the mountaintop each time I feel His presence or witness His hand in my life. This is a place of such indescribable exhilaration and intensity that I long to pitch a tent and live there forever. I treasure moments of emotional oneness with God and view them as a tantalizing glimpse of what is in store for us in heaven.

He laughs with me: Did you realize that God has a clever sense of humor? I have had the opportunity to appreciate it on more than one occasion. One such event occurred in September 2004. My family is extremely close, and we take advantage of every possible opportunity to get together as a group to enjoy a good meal and fellowship. Holidays, birthdays, any occasion will do. Now the joy of being together as a family had become bittersweet for me because of Stephen's absence. His arrival among us had always been met with squeals of delight and great displays of affection. He would enter the room with a big smile and hugs for everyone. On Labor Day we gathered at my mother's home for a family cookout. I found my gaze continuously turning towards the door, waiting for someone who would never arrive. It was difficult, but I managed to maintain my composure and get through the day.

Later that evening after we returned home, my husband left for a few minutes to pick up a newspaper. Finding myself momentarily alone, I decided to spend some time with God, seeking His reassurance and comfort. I knelt by my bed and expressed to Him my longing for Stephen. I told Him how much it hurt to be without him; I prayed for strength and for a tangible sign of His presence to comfort me. I even expressed my certainty that He would provide one before morning.

God knows the intent within my heart. I wasn't trying to test Him or confirm to myself that my faith was well placed. Rather, it was a heartfelt cry for comfort, much like the way a hurt child seeks its Mother. I needed my God and I knew He was there for me.

As I prayed, tears began to fall. Hearing my husband's key in the lock, I hurried to my feet, not wanting him to return and find me crying yet again, and began washing my face in the bathroom. I heard him cross our bedroom and place his keys on his dresser. Then he walked behind me and into the closet. As he passed by, he unconsciously began singing a song he had just heard on the radio. I became completely still and strained to hear. Unbelievably, he was singing the classic "I'll Be There." Motionless, I listened in wonder as he sang, "I'll be there. I'll be there. Just call my name and I'll be there."

He sang only those four lines and nothing more.

By the time he reached the last word, my tears had disappeared and I had buried my face in a hand towel to conceal my laughter. I couldn't tell him at first. This was a secret I wanted to relish privately for just a moment with God, a time of sweet communication between the two of us. A few days later, I finally shared with Jasper how God had used him to console me. Isn't God amazing?

As you grow in Christ, you will learn to more easily recognize His voice. At first I questioned everything. Was that God? What if it was just my own thoughts and I was operating under my own delusions?

I wish I could explain it more fully. Just be patient and trust Him. He will teach you and provide you with what you need to understand Him.

I encourage you to talk to God constantly and study His Word at every opportunity. You will develop discernment and understanding of His will for your life. As you study you are likely to encounter teachers whose interpretations of scripture differ somewhat from what you feel God is saying to you. Don't accept everything you hear from other Christians as God's Word. We are unfortunately fallible and may say things in error or espouse our own opinion as fact. If you encounter a seeming contradiction in theology, seek confirmation in the scriptures. Allow God's Word to serve as your ultimate authority, not another human being. Other people are likely to disappoint you.

As you focus on sharing your faith with others, expect Satan to place obstacles in your path. You may not always receive the affirmation and support you would like. I pray that you do not allow another person to dampen your enthusiasm. Some people will be strongly encouraging; others open and receptive; and others indifferent. It may even be a well-intentioned Christian who inadvertently hurts your feelings or raises questions in your mind about what you believe God has said to you. Know that your relationship with God is your own special experience. It is not dependent upon whether or not anyone else accepts it, believes it, or understands it. Rely upon Him only.

Additionally, you may find yourself suddenly fighting doubts and insecurities from within. Each time I step out in faith, Satan rolls into action. He delights in undermining my confidence with whispered objections such as: *Don't do that. People will think you are crazy. They don't want to hear about God. This is not the appropriate setting for that. You think you are special, don't you? You are just bragging,* and on and on and on.

These arguments may contain just a grain of truth, just enough to cause us to pause and wonder if we should proceed. Our objective is to present ourselves in a way that radiates Christ in our lives and draws others to Him. We should consider our listeners, the content and timing of the message, and the intent within our hearts. Evaluate these factors. You are an ambassador of God and that is an important role. However, don't let these objections paralyze you into inaction.

Consider the alternative arguments:

Undoubtedly, our world is hurting and sliding into moral decline. We are in desperate need of professional leaders in the secular world who are willing to boldly proclaim the "crazy" things God has done for them! We need "normal" people saying "insane" things. It is easy to dismiss the wild-eyed person handing out tracts on the street corner, who looks or dresses differently from us, as being a "religious nut." It is almost impossible to ignore the person who is proclaiming that "God is indeed Lord of all" when this individual is a respected leader in the community. Someone with professional credibility who is willing to boldly proclaim, "I have witnessed God's hand in my life and I place my complete faith in His guidance" gets attention.

In my professional life, I am witnessing an unprecedented emphasis on spirituality. I am far from being the only one using every opportunity I get to declare the eternal truth of our Almighty God. In the past year I have attended two human resource conferences, and at both I was delighted to hear presenters blend their personal faith in their programs. I intentionally sought out two of them afterwards to express my appreciation for their courage in expressing their beliefs and to encourage them to continue. Although I spoke with them individually, their response was the same, "This is who I am and God is too important in my life for me to exclude Him from what I do." I have attended these conferences for the past ten years and have never before heard a presentation that included a testimony of Christian faith.

In business meetings, the topic of Christianity is raised repeatedly. God is truly moving in our society in new and amazing ways. And He invites us to be a part of it! Doesn't it make you want to shout?

So what of the "bragging" consideration? Every relationship with God that has reached a point of deep intimacy shares an identical component. To the person involved, it feels as though he or she is the only person who has ever experienced God in such an extraordinary way. The communication is so intense, so personal, and for lack of an adequate word, just so special! That is okay! The spectacular wonder of it all is that everyone is equally special. Your relationship with God does not detract one bit from another's relationship with Him.

Human relationships often breed jealousy. Not so with God. Christians love to hear what God is doing in the lives of others. We encourage one another and delight in sharing Him. Behold our awesome God!

Search your heart and ask God to remove any personal pride from your testimony. If your intent is purely to express His glory, then tell your story! Share how special and unique He makes you feel. You may stir a hunger within someone else who desperately longs to feel valued and needs to experience his or her own "special" relationship with God.

God may use you to encourage someone else experiencing pain or trauma, someone who is longing to hear your message of deliverance. We have become such a self-absorbed society. Viewed from my perspective, personal trials seem a great deal more challenging than those faced by others. If I hear someone proclaiming God's wonders, I want details. Give me assurance so I will know that His power is great enough to help me too. From what trials have you been rescued? Lacking information, my tendency is to diminish the problems of others so that mine tower in comparison. I tell myself that while God may have been able to manage another's problem, mine is much, much worse. Tell me of your deliverance. I need to hear it. My challenges require a God who is huge!

My friend, God is huge! Share His awesome glory with everyone! They are aching to hear it. As God's people, we must step up. Our generation has become adept at compartmentalizing our lives. We clothe ourselves in one persona for work, one for home, and another for church.

God doesn't fit into that box! He is more than a Sunday morning feel-good experience or your ace-in-the-hole when you die. If you profess Him to be your Savior on Sunday, then I encourage you to live as though you believe He is your Savior every minute of Monday through Saturday as well.

We cannot allow Satan to paralyze us with the fear of what others will think. Scripture tells us in 1 Corinthians 1:18: "For the message of the cross is foolishness to those who are perishing, but to us who are being saved it is the power of God."

While I am not suggesting that you be insensitive to your listener or unprepared in what you plan to say, God does not commission you to water down your testimony to make it more socially acceptable. He tells you to proclaim His truth, His love, and His salvation to the world. I feel strongly that you should prepare. Write down your testimony and practice how to concisely, yet meaningfully, share what God has done in your life. Anticipate and be sensitive to the potential impact of your words on others. However, remember that your job is not to convict or to manipulate them into believing. Your job is simply to share Him accurately and often. The Holy Spirit is quite capable of taking it from there.

Trust Him and relinquish the need to control everything. If we will simply pause for a moment in our hectic existence and gaze in wonder at God's magnificent creation, therein lies enough assurance that His wisdom far surpasses our own. His grace is sufficient to manage any situation.

I encourage you to relish in your salvation. A relationship with God is powerful! It transcends any relationship we could ever have. It is emotional, wonderful, and passionate. I am convinced that if you intentionally and constantly seek God; if you talk to Him throughout the day, while you are working, going to school, driving your car, shopping for groceries; if you invite Him to be with you every minute of every day, you can live on the mountaintop.

David is described in the Bible as a man after God's own heart.

In 2 Samuel 6:14-15 we find a description of King David as he brought the ark of God to Jerusalem. "David, wearing a linen ephod, danced before the Lord with all his might, while he and the entire house of Israel brought up the ark of the Lord with shouts and the sound of trumpets." David was consistently passionate and emotional about his God, and if that sort of behavior resulted in God being delighted in him, that is good enough for me!

My prayer for myself, and for you as well, is that we experience the same fervor and excitement about walking with God which spurred David to dance through the streets of Jerusalem. While I may be the least coordinated among us and my feet may refuse to cooperate, my heart has surely learned to dance.

Praise be to the God
and Father of our Lord Jesus Christ,
the Father of compassion
and the God of all comfort,
who comforts us in all our troubles,
so that we can comfort
those in any trouble
with the comfort we ourselves
have received from God.
2 Corinthians 1:3-4

Chapter 12

More Like Jesus

As I began to study the Bible, I found example after example of God pouring out His compassion upon those who are grieving. I wonder if this stems from the fact that when Adam and Eve were created, they were never intended to die. We were meant to live in complete love and fellowship with God. However, Satan and our rebellious nature intervened and thus death was introduced to the world.

While growing up I mercifully had little personal experience with death, but when I did, I reacted forcefully. I was nine years old and in the third grade when one of my great grandmothers passed away. I had only met her once years before and couldn't recall anything about her, but I did remember sitting on a small stone donkey she had in her yard. I was preparing for school one morning when we received a call notifying us of her death.

I left for school, but once I was in my classroom I became so distraught that I had to be taken to the nurse's office where I lay down until my grandmother arrived to pick me up. I spent the rest of the day in bed crying. I did not know her personally, so my grief did not stem from personal loss or from fear. I believe it was more an inner certainty that death is just horribly wrong.

God believes that death is wrong as well, and through the sacrifice of His Son, Jesus Christ, death was defeated for all time.

One example of God's amazing compassion that never ceases to thrill my heart every time I read it is recorded in Luke 7:11-15. Jesus and His disciples, followed by a large crowd, were entering the city when they passed a funeral procession headed in the opposite direction. A widow had just lost her only son. The mother, absorbed in her own personal nightmare, did not look at Jesus as they passed. She did not seek Him out or plead with Him to help her. Yet He saw the agony within her heart. His heart was moved by her anguish. "Don't cry," He told her. Then He placed his hands upon the body of her son and said, "Young man, I say to you, get up!" The boy was instantly restored to life, and Scripture reads that "Jesus gave him back to his mother." He cares!

Another well-known example is recorded in John Chapter 11. This account describes how Lazarus became ill and how his sisters sent word to Jesus that, unless He came to them immediately, His dear friend would die. Jesus deliberately tarried, and by the time He arrived, Lazarus had been dead for four days. When Jesus was told of his death and witnessed the grieving of those who loved Lazarus, Scripture tells us in verse 33 that He was deeply moved in spirit and troubled. In verse 35 we read that Jesus wept. How reassuring those words have been to me. Jesus loved Lazarus, and although He knew that within minutes He would restore life to his body, Jesus experienced grief and He wept. Although I believe with all of my heart that I will be reunited with Stephen, I miss him now and I weep. God understands!

Yet another account that touches my heart is during the last few moments of His crucifixion. As Jesus hung dying on the cross and becoming, through His sacrifice, a bridge to God for all mankind, He responded to the personal agony of His mother. Although Mary accepted God's plan for the son to whom she had given birth, her misery was multiplied exponentially. Her Savior was being cruci-fied, but He was also her child whom she had raised and loved, the boy she held in her arms and comforted when He cried. In John 19:26, the disciple known as the "one whom He loved" records the words Jesus spoke to comfort His mother. Verses 26-27 read, "'...Dear woman, here is your son,' and to the disciple, 'Here is your mother.'" In the midst of His own agony, Jesus responded to her anguish and ensured that John would be there to care for her and to comfort her.

I shared with you previously how God used the name Norbert to get my attention in the month immediately following Stephen's death. Approximately six months later I began thinking about this incident again. Although I had no idea why, I felt that there was much more to this situation than I yet realized. I continued to contemplate it overnight, and the very next day I received an employment verification form for the associate named Norbert who had worked for my company. I reviewed his file, looking for anything to explain the odd connection I had to this young man whom I had never met personally.

I could find nothing at all until I checked the references we had recorded for him. We had received a written response from an indi-vidual who had signed the reference "J. Barker." *That is interesting,* I thought. My dad's name is James Barker.

This event served to heighten my interest and I began to feel quite strongly that I needed to view the movie that had originally caught my attention because of the connection to my dream. I could not remember the name of the movie, but I could remember the plot. I thought of contacting the television station but convinced myself that it was probably a made-for-TV movie and I would never be able to get my hands on a copy of it.

On Sunday, January 30, 2005, God's faithfulness was again revealed to me. In South Carolina we were experiencing one of our few ice storms of the season. Church had been cancelled due to the weather, so that afternoon I was reading the Sunday school lesson that I had missed that morning. Meanwhile, my husband, Jasper, watched a movie in our bedroom. Unexpectedly, I began craving an ice cream sundae and, since the weather had grown warmer and melted the ice, I suggested that we go to TCBY and use a gift certificate I had received for Christmas. This was not something we did on a regular basis, and it seemed particularly unusual since it was cold outside and we had just experienced an ice storm! Not one to question his wife's unpredictable cravings, Jasper agreed and began to get ready. Realizing that the movie he was watching should be almost finished, I went into our bedroom to look for the gift certificate. Just as I entered the room, I heard an announcement on the television that coming up next was the movie "Ticker," a story set in San Francisco involving terrorists who threatened to blow up the city.

Jasper must have thought I had lost my mind, because I began running around looking for a blank videotape, stammering, "That is the Norbert movie! That is it! I have to record it. It comes on in fifteen minutes!"

I found a videotape, inserted it into the VCR upstairs to record the movie, and then called my mother and Michael to tell them that the "Norbert movie" was about to begin. I set the tape to record and then sat riveted to the television screen, waiting to confirm that I had indeed seen the name Norbert a year before. It was there! I was elated and had to tear myself away to go to TCBY. I recorded the movie because we would be leaving to attend the evening worship service at our church before it ended, and I wanted to watch the entire movie at one time. I was not going to chance missing whatever significance it might hold for me.

After church Jasper and I sat down in the living room to watch the movie. I discovered that when I set the VCR to record, it had also recorded the last few minutes of the movie that immediately preceded "Ticker." It was a Nicholas Cage movie called "Con Air." The first words spoken after the tape began rolling were by an actress who said, "Hello, Cameron."

I jumped from the sofa. "What did she say?" I rewound the tape and listened intently. There it was again, "Hello, Cameron."

Several years previously, Stephen had suddenly raised the idea of changing his name. The name he selected was Kameron Glass. Although he never actually changed his name legally, he did research the process and used this name for his email account.

"Okay, God," I thought, "this is getting off to an interesting start." Within minutes I was sitting in complete amazement. The movie "Ticker" begins with a hostage situation and a SWAT team running into position outside of a mansion. In the midst of the chaos of flashing lights, explosions, and helicopters, the camera suddenly zooms in for an extremely close-up shot of a name embroidered on the front of a shirt. The name was GLASS.

As the movie progressed, it became apparent that the subplot of the movie surrounded a detective who had recently lost his wife and son and his struggle to accept their deaths. Steven Seagal plays a bomb expert named Glass who counsels the detective as they work on the case together.

Glass urges the grieving detective to accept that death is not the end. He assures him that he will see his loved ones again, and in the final scene of the movie, Glass encourages the detective to talk to them because his love for them is eternal and so are they.

I am uncertain how long I sat there motionless after the movie ended, crying at the faithfulness of God. So many details had to come together to speak to me in this way. Events had been set in motion years ago, even before I had the need to see them.

Undoubtedly, God spoke to us through this movie intentionally and quite deliberately. We felt that He had literally stepped into our living room and pulled up a chair.

I wondered at God's reasons for providing closure regarding the Norbert saga. I was overjoyed that He chose to make His presence so obvious to me. However, I already trusted Him and believed in Him completely. I wasn't drawn closer to Him by this event because I was already there. But then I realized that my husband, Jasper, had been drawn closer to God from this occurrence. Witnessing this event provided him with all that he needed to acknowledge God's active presence in our lives.

The results of the change within his heart became evident six weeks later. For months I had been telling Jasper that I wanted to join the church we were attending, but he wasn't ready. Each week, when the invitation was made at the end of the service, it became an ordeal for me to sit in the pew rather than to heed God's call on my heart to step forward. There was no doubt in my mind that God was leading me in this direction. However, I did not want to join without my husband. Tension over this issue was building a wall between us. The more I pleaded and argued, the more strenuously he resisted.

My urgency to join stemmed from the burden God had placed within my heart to become involved in His ministry. I felt a deep desire to share with others the wonder of living in close communication with God. I wanted everyone to experience the same comfort, joy, and peace He had brought into my life. There are so many hurting people in the world, and I felt that I could help by sharing what I had learned. The best place to start was within my own church. However, I knew that I needed to be a member to participate in the way I felt led to be involved.

A few weeks after the Norbert incident, I attended the last night of our revival service alone and feeling deeply disturbed. I struggled to suppress my negative thoughts and focus instead on the young lady who stepped onto the stage to sing. She sang with skill and genuine feeling, and as I listened to her lovely voice carrying the message, "It is well with my soul," I felt my cares dissolve. God had brought me so far in this journey, and I realized in that moment with complete certainty that if I never again saw His hand so obviously revealed in my life, all was truly well with my soul.

This church service had restored my joy, but the next evening I once again found my mind caught in the dilemma over joining the church. Following dinner at a local restaurant, Jasper had work to complete at his office, so I drove home alone. Once inside I went upstairs to Stephen's room to pray. I expressed my confusion to God. I felt confident that I knew His will on this issue yet didn't understand in which direction to turn. Should I join without Jasper and by my choice risk driving him away from God? Or should I wait until he was ready despite feeling that I was living in disobedience to God? I cried, praying for a clear answer that would leave no doubt as to the path I should follow.

I prepared for bed and considered looking for an answer within the Bible. *No,* I thought, *I am not likely to hear anything so direct as "this is what you should do when your husband is not ready to join the church and you are," and I need a precise response to that question.* Instead I opted for Christian television.

The first words I heard spoken when I turned on the TV were from the host of the show. She asked her guest if he was available to speak at churches within the area and share his story. He responded that he was, and then he began to relate how his wife had accepted Christ first and then led him to the Lord by never once judging him, nagging him, or pressuring him about his own salvation. She loved him right into the arms of God.

I said, "Oh my! That was quick!"

I considered what I had just heard. "God, I think I hear what You are telling me, but since I feel so powerfully convicted about this issue, I want to be sure. Will You confirm it for me?" Within minutes, the host introduced the next segment. The same young man stepped onto the stage and began to sing "It Is Well With My Soul."

That settled the issue in my mind, and when Jasper returned home a short time later, I told him that I had prayed about our conflict and would not pressure him any longer about joining the church. I told him that I trusted his heart, and that I knew he was not trying to hurt me by delaying, and that I would wait as long as I could. I believed that he would do the right thing at the right time.

Eleven days later we were sitting in church listening to our pastor preach a sermon from Genesis 22, the account of Abraham and Isaac. Although I had spoken of this to no one except God, in my mind I had compared my situation to Abraham and his willing-ness to give up his son. It seemed to me that although my loss had not required my willing participation as with Abraham, the sacrifice of my son had precipitated the birth of my faith in God. I wondered during the sermon if the selection of this topic was intended to mean anything significant to me on this particular day.

I waited eagerly as the invitation began, but when my husband did not move, I decided I had misread the signs. With my eyes still closed I prayed, "God, it doesn't have to be today. I know that Your plan will be accomplished in my life, and I will wait." Just then I felt Jasper touch my arm. I opened my eyes and he smiled, saying, "Let's go." He took my arm and together we walked down the aisle to join the church. Not only that, but later that day we submitted a deposit to join a group from our church on a trip to Israel in November.

I realize that God may not always respond to prayer so instantly or so obviously in my life. However, I believe that as long as my prayers are focused upon identifying His will, combined with a strong desire to follow His call whatever it may be, He will provide the answers I need to do so.

Jesus replied, "I tell you the truth,
if you have faith and do not doubt,
not only can you do what was done to the fig tree,
but also you can say to this mountain,
'Go, throw yourself into the sea,'
and it will be done."
Matthew 21:21

Now faith is being sure of what we hope for
and certain of what we do not see.
Hebrews 11:1

Chapter 13

Trees Wear Glasses, Don't They?

When Stephen and Michael were young children and experiencing my rebuke for some mischief they had gotten themselves into, they would gaze back at me with wide-eyed, innocent smiles and respond with, "Well, you *borned* us!" It was impossible for me to suppress my own grin, and inevitably my annoyance would quickly dissolve into laughter.

One day recently I found myself apologizing to God for my not possessing a certain skill or talent that I wished I could use for His glory in the same way I had seen demonstrated by others. Suddenly, I stopped and smiled towards heaven. "Wait just a minute," I said, "You *borned* me!"

God is intimately familiar with my strengths and weaknesses. He formed me and knit me together in my mother's womb. He assembled within me the exact combination of abilities that He wanted me to have, those required to support His plan for my life. And He did the same thing for you. Appreciate the talents of others, but understand that yours are equally important. You were intentionally and carefully designed for a purpose, His purpose – not your own. Consider your natural passions and abilities and then ask God to tell you how He intended them to be used in His service. Beseech Him for guidance and implore Him to create opportunities for you. God seeks a surrendered and willing heart. If you offer yourself to Him in this way, He will certainly provide the rest!

God's grace and strength is sufficient to empower you to conquer any obstacle, even when the obstacle lies within yourself and seems embedded within your personality. Ask anyone you know to describe the type of situation that tends to cause them the greatest discomfort, and the response you are likely to hear is being asked to speak in front of a group. The fear of public speaking is almost universal. Even those who do so frequently can easily remember their struggle to overcome the physical symptoms of stage fright: butterflies in the stomach, shaking hands, perspiration, and dry mouth.

As a young career woman, it was imperative that I learn to manage my fear in order to be accepted as a credible professional. Eventually through practice I gained some measure of control over the evidence of these feelings, but I always battled mightily with the feelings themselves. I would awaken on any morning that I was to deliver a presentation with a sinking feeling in my stomach, asking myself, "Debbie, why do you do this to yourself? You could sit there quietly in the audience and enjoy the show like everyone else instead of torturing yourself this way." Yet, some irrational force seemed to pull me towards these situations despite my inner desire to flee!

A few months before Stephen died I had been asked to serve as President-elect and then President of our Greenwood Chamber of Commerce in 2005. My first thought was not of the prestige involved or even of the potential business benefits that might result from such a position. Quite literally, my first thought was, *If I accept this position, in just over a year, I must speak as incoming president to a group of approximately 500 people at the annual meeting.* The idea filled me with terror but, since I had a long time to prepare, I decided to take the plunge and hope for the best. My doubts stemmed from my dependence upon my own abilities to carry me through the challenge. It never occurred to me to ask God for assistance. After all, I was the one who had done all of the work and made sure that I was ideally positioned to be asked to serve as a leader.

Who was I kidding? Deep inside and only to myself, I marveled at all of the blessings and opportunities that came my way without any intentional planning on my part. However, I felt little inclination to examine the topic of my unworthiness too closely.

At first after Stephen died, I had withdrawn from many of my public responsibilities and considered resigning from the Chamber position as well. I knew that everyone would understand. But something stopped me. I sensed, without understanding why, that I was supposed to do this, that somehow this opportunity was the culmination of my professional achievements thus far and part of a much bigger plan.

As God drew me to Him in the year between Stephen's death and the date of the annual meeting, I began to understand that the persistent voice of truth within my heart had been correct all along. I admitted that I had been brought to this place in my life by God and not as a result of my own initiative or by chance. He knew how my soul would be shattered from losing my dear son; but He also understood that the new person who would emerge from that rubble would be totally surrendered to Him. I first reached for Him in desperation, then I clung to Him in gratitude, and finally I yielded to Him in complete reverence and love. My visibility within our community had a purpose. It would be used for His glory.

As the evening of the big event drew near, I was astonished by the sense of peace and anticipation that filled my heart regarding my speech. *Where is the usual terror?* I wondered. *Debbie, have you forgotten there will be five hundred people present?* I sat very still in my office, in my car, and at home examining my heart and then my stomach, looking for butterflies, but there was not a one. How fascinating! Perhaps, I told myself, I was in denial and the morning of the speech I would awaken to that familiar sick feeling of inadequacy, just as I had every other time. But somehow I knew better.

The theme and main ideas for the speech had come to mind effortlessly a few months earlier. Since I had not even begun planning for the annual meeting when the idea came to me, I questioned God thinking He intended it to be included in this book. It just didn't fit! The truth struck me suddenly a few weeks after preparing the outline that this was not intended as a chapter for the book but was rather my speech for the Chamber! It contained a blend of humor, business, and most importantly, faith.

Remember my point a few paragraphs back? He *borned* me! Well, whenever He gets frustrated at my lack of understanding, which I'm sure I provide Him with ample opportunity to do so, I hope He remembers that He made me this way!

The morning of the speech dawned beautiful and clear. As I prepared for work, I felt no misgivings. Instead I was flooded with a sense of exhilaration that today I would have the opportunity to show many others the living evidence of God's tremendous power in my life. Most would have heard of the tragic loss of my son and might be expecting to see a woman broken by pain and struggling to survive. I prayed that they would not see that in me. I wanted to show them a woman vibrant with the light of God burning within her. I wanted them to question from where I drew the strength required to carry on, and then I wanted to point them towards the source, my wonderful Lord and Savior.

The moment for me to take the stage neared and I silently quoted Psalm 40, reminding myself of the purpose behind all I had experienced. As my mind lingered on each word, I felt my soul swell with a confidence and power I had never before experienced. I stood, strode confidently to the stage, and delivered a speech before what would normally have been an intimidating crowd of people. I felt as comfortable as I would if speaking to a small group of friends in my living room. The response was overwhelmingly positive.

Friends, I have delivered presentations before and I can tell you that, without a doubt, God made the difference! I basically just stood in the right place and He did the rest. Many times that is all He asks of any of us: "Just do as I say and trust Me, regardless of your doubts and fears. Stand there and watch Me work!"

It was awesome. If He never again uses me in that way, it was enough for me to experience it once. Have you heard people claim to be in their zone when intently focused on doing something they enjoy? There is no zone like God's zone! To feel as though all of your personal desires and passions come together in one moment, uniting with God to accomplish good for His kingdom, is sheer ecstasy, or at least the closest we can get to it on earth.

I am certain you have wondered about the title of this book, "Trees Wear Glasses, Don't They?" Obviously, trees don't wear glasses, and what does such a nonsensical statement have to do with anything related to loss or to our Lord, anyway?

Friend, I have personally discovered and pray that I have adequately shared with you that our amazing God speaks to us in many ways and through any number of unusual tools. So often He has touched my heart with ordinary things that He used in extraordinary ways. There was one event in particular that marked the turning point in my relationship with Him because it involved my decision to relinquish control of my life to Him. I honor this moment because it was the precise second that I understood and recognized the full extent of my commitment to Him, and that has made all the difference in the world.

The day was a beautiful Saturday afternoon in June. We were expecting family for dinner, and in preparation for their arrival I stepped outside to sweep the front steps. I had just finished and was turning to go inside when an odd sight caught my attention. Just to my right near the corner of the house, lying starkly white against the emerald green of the grass, was a big pile of feathers. I dropped the broom and approached them, worried that one of the wild geese that inhabited the pond in front of our house had been attacked and might be laying there injured. Relieved, I saw that there was no sign of blood or disturbance of any kind. Just a big pile of long feathers, perhaps two or three handfuls.

Now I was really puzzled. What could have caused such a thing? I glanced at the tree directly in front of the feathers, wondering if there was a nest of some kind in there. The tree is an arborvitae, a smooth evergreen with a cylindrical shape, tapering at the top with densely packed flat needles and standing approximately twelve feet tall. My eyes were scanning it quickly from top to bottom, seeking an explanation, when suddenly they stopped abruptly.

All thoughts of feathers were driven from my mind as I stood transfixed by the black-framed glasses that stared hollowly back at me from the tree. They were resting there among the greenery, perfectly at my eye level, and seemed to be returning my astonished expression. *That tree is wearing glasses and is looking at me.* I stood frozen in place and almost felt something click deep within my mind. I took a deep breath and decided, *Okay. Trees wear glasses now. If God wants trees to wear glasses from this day forward, I can incorporate that into my reality.*

I smiled, content with that decision, and began to walk back towards the house when the voice of reason interrupted and politely suggested that I consider giving my conclusion a little more thought. I hesitated, then turned and retrieved the glasses from their curious position among the branches. Admittedly, there was probably a reasonable explanation. Returning inside, I showed the glasses to Jasper and shared with him how I had discovered them. Laughing, he identified them as a pair of reading glasses he had misplaced. We determined that he had left them outside and one of the neighborhood children must have put them in the tree as a joke.

It was such a small prank and probably long forgotten by the person who did it, yet it held such profound and lasting implications for me. The realization hit me immediately that I had reached a point from which there was no turning back, not that I wanted to. God had become Lord of my life completely. This event revealed to me that I would willingly accept anything He presented to me with an open and grateful heart. I don't have to understand it. I don't even have to like it.

I pray that each of you experience such a moment! Do trees wear glasses? Yes, if God says they do!

Do miracles still happen? I have witnessed them!

Will the sky roll back at the sound of a trumpet and a victorious shout at the moment our Savior returns to redeem His own? Oh, yes!

And will a brokenhearted mom once again caress the beautiful face of her son and hold him in her arms, never again having to let him go? I am willing to stake my life on it!

I praise God for what He has done for Stephen and through my life as a result of my deeply rooted love for that child. God had to break me in order for me to understand that I was nothing on my own, and that life only became worth living the moment I sincerely invited Him to walk beside me, to lead me, and to share every moment of it with me.

There is a powerful lesson for all of us to learn from my walk through the valley. God literally lifted me from the pit of death, set me on a firm path, and gave me a new song to sing. And I will proclaim it boldly to anyone who will listen. I want to be an empty vessel for God to use, for His words to ring through me and touch the hearts of others, to change other lives just as He has changed mine. Forget me. It won't bother me if you don't remember my name. Just remember seeing Him within me.

God has a calling on your life as well. He wants none to perish and will attempt to turn your heart to Him through every means possible. I hope that you will not encounter His grace through pain and brokenness as I have, but if that method is the only one that will get your attention, know that His love is sufficient to carry you through it.

Scripture has come alive for me in more ways than I can convey. In Jeremiah 29:12-13, God tells us, "Then you will call upon me and come and pray to me, and I will listen to you. You will seek me and find me when you seek me with all your heart." That promise is real! As I have reached for Him, He has responded.

I am not referring to making a one-time commitment to God and then returning to life as you knew it. Every morning I make a deliberate choice to commit that day to God. And as I seek His presence, He reveals Himself more frequently and more obviously to me. He wants all of you, every part, and in return will fill you with almost more of Himself than you can safely bear.

Are you seeking fulfillment in life? Have you tried to find it in career success, wealth, relationships, drugs, alcohol, and promiscuity? It is like chasing the wind, living without God. Contentment is always just beyond reach and never attainable. I experienced this in building my business. I sought recognition and financial success, and each achievement left me empty and reaching for the next one. I could never get there.

I have it now, a life bursting with contentment, joy, and great anticipation; a life completely devoid of fear. Do you have that? Can you even imagine it? Do you lay awake at night worried about mistakes you have made or of what the future will hold for you? I did, and I considered myself to be a reasonably confident and optimistic person. When you put your trust in God and believe with all of your heart that He loves you, the chains of fear are loosened and fall harmlessly to the ground. As Scripture tells us, when you are free in Christ, you are free indeed.

So can you believe with complete faith? Do trees wear glasses in your heart? If you haven't made that decision yet, there is no better time than now. We will wait for you. Stop right now and acknowledge to God that you are a sinner who will perish without Him, and that you need Him to become Lord of your life. Ask for forgiveness and accept the gift of salvation He extends to you through Jesus and His death upon the cross.

Do you need to recommit your life to Christ? He is waiting to accept you and welcome you back to His family regardless of anything you may have done while you strayed. Use this time to examine your faith and ask forgiveness. Resolve to start over today. God will provide you with a blank slate, a do-over. Your new life can begin this very moment.

I praise God for your life and your commitment. I pray that He will use all of us in mighty ways to build His kingdom. Now that we have identified the path to true success while we are on earth, let's turn our attention to something far superior!

Then I saw a new heaven and a new earth,
for the first heaven
and the first earth had passed away,
and there was no longer any sea.
I saw the Holy City, the new Jerusalem,
coming down out of heaven from God,
prepared as a bride
beautifully dressed for her husband.
And I heard a loud voice from the throne saying,
"Now the dwelling of God is with men,
and he will live with them.
They will be his people,
and God himself will be with them
and be their God.
He will wipe every tear from their eyes.
There will be no more death
or mourning or crying or pain,
for the old order of things has passed away."
Revelation 21:1-4

Chapter 14

The Beginning

Stephen was born on August 30, 1982. As his birthday approached, I decided that placing flowers in the church on Sunday, August 29, would be a loving way to honor his memory and to recognize that special day. I wanted the arrangement to be truly special, a floral representation of the love and promise God had brought into our lives. Not having a creative bone in my body when it comes to flowers, I also felt completely lost as to where to begin.

One morning I was contemplating the arrangement as I drove to work, when suddenly I recalled hearing a sermon long ago that had referenced the colors of heaven. I seemed to remember that the scripture passage could be found in the book of Revelation and I drove a little faster, anxious to reach my office and search my Bible to verify my memory.

Once there, I thumbed hurriedly through the pages, scanning them quickly, searching for any reference to colors. When I came upon Revelation 21, the passage quoted above, I stopped. These words spoke directly to my heart. As I continued reading further into the passage, I discovered beginning with verse 18 a glowing depiction of the gemstones that form the foundation of heaven. *Gemstones are specific colors*, I told myself. This was it! I instantly recognized these words to be the floral blueprint for the arrangement God had placed in my heart. Originally my idea had been simply to ask the florist to select flowers in the same colors as those mentioned in the Bible. Yet, when I read these particular verses, that vision changed. I had no idea how this concept could be translated into a floral arrangement but I trusted that somehow it would be done.

Not only would this arrangement serve to honor Stephen's birthday; it would also reach beyond our family and friends and speak to the hearts of everyone who saw it, especially those who had lost loved ones. We could gaze upon it and imagine those we loved walking in the presence of God and surrounded by the beauty of those colors. This visualization would bring comfort to our pain and fuel the anticipation of one day joining them in that beautiful heavenly place.

I readily acknowledge that this idea extended far beyond anything I could have imagined on my own. That awareness, combined with the conviction that this decision was divinely right, convinced me that God was leading me step by step along the way. I copied the verses and drove to the florist to share my idea. The florist we had used for Stephen's funeral was someone I did not know well. Kitty was a good friend of Stephen's dad, Rick, and he had expressed his desire to use her company, Candlelight Creations, on that day. Somehow, I knew she was the one to mold this dream into a reality.

As I entered her shop, I noticed that she was on the telephone so I took the opportunity to browse. I wandered over to a corner where several specialty items were displayed. I examined one item and then another while I waited for her telephone call to end. Suddenly, I froze, blinking back the tears that threatened to spill from my eyes. There before me, hanging innocently on the wall, was a personal confirmation from God.

When Kitty selected this assortment of copper cookie cutters for her shop, I am certain that she had no idea that God's hand was in that decision. Yet, there displayed among all of the individually packaged cookie cutters was a single set. The set contained the outline of a hand and in the middle of the hand was a separate cookie cutter in the shape of a heart. My thoughts instantly turned to the prayer I had shared with my Rotary Club just a few short weeks before. Remember the sentence that was such a struggle for me to speak without tears? "Father, you know that from the day Stephen was born, he held my heart in his hands." Those words, which described my deepest feelings for my son, had been translated into a tangible reality. Didn't that coincide perfectly with the purpose of my visit to this shop? I shared a smile with God as I picked them up, knowing that this was one purchase I would surely treasure forever.

As I described the concept for the arrangement to Kitty, I saw her eyes begin to glow. I could glimpse the excitement building within her as her mind evaluated the various options available. By the time I left her shop, I felt completely confident that God would again guide her hand, especially when I discovered that she also attended Rice Memorial Baptist Church. I had not realized that we attended the same church since she attended the early morning service and we always attended the later service.

The day finally arrived, and the arrangement was displayed in all of its splendor upon the altar of our church. Included within the bulletin that day was a separate insert with the text from Revelation 21:1-4 and 19-21 quoted so that everyone in attendance would be aware of and understand the significance of the arrangement.

Revelation 21:19-21 reads:

The foundations of the city walls were decorated with every kind of precious stone. The first foundation was jasper, the second sapphire, the third chalcedony, the fourth emerald, the fifth sardonyx, the sixth carnelian, the seventh chrysolite, the eighth beryl, the ninth topaz, the tenth chrysoprase, the eleventh jacinth, and the twelfth amethyst. The twelve gates were twelve pearls, each gate made of a single pearl. The great street of the city was of pure gold, like transparent glass.

While it is impossible to convey the beauty of Kitty's creation in words, I will attempt to describe how she chose to depict heaven with flowers. She began the project by painstakingly researching the colors of the stones that formed each layer of the foundation. Then, using silk flowers, she packed them tightly together in row upon row of brilliant color, gradually decreasing them in vertical width. Upon each row she fastened translucent stones in the identical colors as the flowers to glisten and reflect the light. Near the top she attached curving gates that she had fashioned from artificial pearls. Weaving below and then through the gate, she used shiny golden fabric to depict the streets of gold. Finally, crowning the top stood a porcelain figure of Jesus with his eyes and hands raised towards heaven. The end result was stunning.

I watched in wonder that Sunday morning as members of the congregation entered the church and opened their bulletins. Their eyes were immediately drawn to the altar, and I could see them reading and then glancing back and forth from the arrangement to God's Word, matching each stone described in Scripture to the color displayed before them. At the end of the service many people approached us to express how deeply they had been touched by our gift to the church. Some had also lost loved ones. Several spoke of how they had never before visualized that passage of Scripture in the same way that they had today. Now they could hold an image in their minds of the glory that awaited us in heaven, a vision that helped to bring those precious words to life in their hearts. One lady who was visiting from a northern state asked if she could take pictures because she wanted to have the arrangement recreated for her church.

I could never have imagined a better way to honor the life of my dear son than for God to use our loss to reach others. What more could I desire than for Stephen to live on through our service and obedience to the Lord who saved him?

The following day, Stephen's actual birthday, I chose to spend the day at home alone with God and with Stephen. I spent the morning praying and listening as God spoke to me through Scripture. It was upon this day that I discovered what has become "my" passage of Scripture, the words borrowed from David in Psalm 40:1-3 which I used to introduce this book. Within those three verses is summarized the story of my life.

During this time we have spent together, through my limited perspective I have described how God has used Stephen's death to transform my life. I want to share with you that the manifestations of His presence and the astounding means with which He chose to open my heart have not only changed my life but also the lives of many others as well.

On the afternoon of Stephen's birthday, Kitty called to see how I was doing and to tell me about an event involving her son and the arrangement she had created for our church. Her little boy, who is four years old, enjoys helping her in her shop. As they prepared to load the arrangement into her car for delivery to the church on Saturday, he suddenly exclaimed, "Mom, you forgot something!" "What did I forget, honey?" she asked. He responded, "The picture of that little boy. You are supposed to put it in the arrangement!" Kitty told him it was there but he was unconvinced, so she was forced to put the heavy arrangement on the ground at his eye level to show him. Unknown to most, since it was hidden from view behind the street of gold, she had positioned a small picture of Stephen. He questioned her concerning the reason the picture was hidden in that location. She explained that Stephen had already entered the gates of heaven so we couldn't see him anymore, but he was there at the feet of Jesus. Satisfied with this explanation, he allowed the arrangement to be placed in the car and appeared to forget about it.

Kitty told me that following the worship service on Sunday her family had joined her parents for lunch. No sooner had they arrived than her son eagerly piped up, "Papa, something really neat happened at church today!" He described for the suddenly attentive group how he and his mom had created an arrangement of heaven for this little boy who had died and how today the boy's mother got to sit in the church and look at it and see her little boy in heaven with Jesus. "Papa," he said, "We hid a picture of him near Jesus behind the street of gold, and guess what? He was smiling!" At four years old, he assumed that the smile on Stephen's face in the picture was the direct result of being with Jesus. Kitty and I both wept as she shared how viewing this arrangement had left an indelible impression of the joy of heaven within the heart of her child, an impression that he would certainly carry with him for the rest of his life. Yes, in the midst of pain, God is exceedingly good!

God has also transformed the lives of many other family members who were close to Stephen, using their grief as the key to enter their broken hearts. Michael, Stephen's brother, has witnessed the evidence of God in our lives throughout this tragedy. My eyes have seen faith blossom in his heart, and it has brought me great joy to witness his initial skepticism being converted into an abiding love and appreciation for our Savior.

Many spiritual wounds have been healed in others whose souls were previously injured by people who claimed to be Christians but who behaved towards them in ungodly ways. I have watched, thankfully, their hurt dissolve as they were drawn back into the arms of God through this experience.

Unfortunately, there remain a few close family members who have not yet accepted Christ as their Savior. Their heartbreak is painful to watch, especially knowing that comfort and redemption lies directly before them just waiting for their acceptance. I pray for them often and seek your prayers for their salvation as well.

In sharing my story with you, I realize that I have focused heavily on my experiences in coming to know God. Let me emphasize that the methods God used to reach my family may not be typical and are very likely to differ from your own experience with Him. Every relationship with God is uniquely amazing and special regardless of the means of communication. I may never again experience Him in the way I have thus far and if so, that is fine with me.

God saved my life, physically and spiritually. The treasure lies not in miraculous encounters with God, but rather in drawing close to Him through personal Bible study, continuous prayer, and pursuing His will for your life. My desire for you is that you seek God Himself and not simply the experience of God.

One desolate night, February 11, 2004, I had cried out in anguish, "Why God? Why did you give me such love for a child, only to take him from me in this way?"

He reached out to me through the darkness to quell the storm that raged within me. I don't claim to know the mind of God or even why such pain is allowed to enter our lives. However, the answers that God has revealed to me and to my family in the past year have been enough.

Stephen made his own choices as he traveled his short path through life, many of which brought sorrow to those who loved him. But during those all too brief years, he eternally captured our hearts. It was God who created the powerful bond that so fiercely connects our hearts to his. While I don't believe God is responsible for the wrong turns Stephen made, I am convinced that He alone has the power to take what Satan has damaged and turn it even more powerfully to His glory.

So, why did this happen? I declare it was because God knew that our love for Stephen would be a driving force in turning us towards Him, saving us from a superficial existence, and transforming us into effective witnesses that could be used to impact the lives of others. Nothing less would have gotten our attention or so radically redirected our paths.

Through our tragedy I have discovered the heart of God. Although I am certain to encounter more pain and difficult challenges during the remainder of my time on this earth, I have become convinced of His goodness, that He deeply cares when we suffer, and that if we had the insight to see our role within the entire picture in the way that He does, we would become more accepting of our trials. When I don't understand or cannot see the hand of God, I will absolutely put my faith in His heart.

I have heard it said that until you no longer fear death, you are unable to truly live.

Friends, let me close by saying that I am unafraid to die. In fact, I eagerly anticipate the glorious day when my work on earth is done and I will meet my Savior face to face. Until then, through the death of my son, God has taught me what it means to truly live. I will take that wisdom and use it to live out His purpose for my life. I present myself at His feet, an offering representing my immeasurable gratitude for the life of my dear son, Stephen Ryan Dropps, and my love for the Lord who will bring us together again.

I vow that Stephen's legacy will not be one of pain and brokenness but rather a legacy of love, comfort, and compassion, guiding others to our caring and merciful God. We ask that you pray for us as God uses our experience to minister to others. May our daily commitment be to reach a desperate and dying world with a boldly ringing call to faith in God.

To order additional copies of:

Trees Wear Glasses, Don't They?
A Call to Faith

or to schedule Debbie Turner
for your next event

visit our website at **www.calltofaith.net**

OR

You may mail a check or money order for $18.00
(Book plus 5% SC sales tax and shipping/handling) to:

Call To Faith Ministry
P.O. Box 50561
Greenwood, SC 29649

Credit card purchases may be made online at
www.xulonpress.com/bookstore
or by calling 1(866) 909-BOOK (2665)

Printed in the United States
34301LVS00005BC/106-255